FOR EVERY SEASON

There is a Pasta

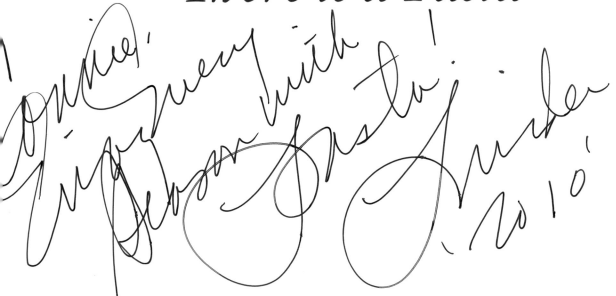

FOR EVERY SEASON

There is a Pasta

LINDA STEIDEL

Photography by Mark Choate

Brio Press
12 South Sixth Street #1250
Minneapolis, Minnesota 55412
www.briobooks.com

Manufactured in the United States of America

10 9 8 7 6 5 4 3 2 1

Edited by Cindy Choate
Book Design by Brio | Anthony Sclavi Minneapolis, MN
Photography: Mark Choate

International Standard Book Number
ISBN 13: 978-0-9826687-6-4
Library of Congress Control Number: 2010935409

First Edition

Acknowledgments

It takes a lot to put a cookbook together. It's a collaboration of many. I love working on the recipes, testing, tasting and writing them. My challenge is to make them do-able, delicious and easy to read. However, what brings them to life is the photography. Mark Choate is my partner and the photographer. The pictures are so beautiful, you feel like you can actually taste the pasta dishes. This is always the goal; Mark makes it happen.

Cindy Choate is my editor and an official taster. We work our way through every dish to the very end. We never give up. We clean our plates!

The team at Brio started out as just our publisher, and they have become our friends. They are all uniquely special. Will guides us with his calm and expertise in all publishing matters. Anthony is the most creative art director. We are so lucky. Sara is a persistent, hard-working publicist and does a great job. Thank you all so much.

'For Every Season There is a Pasta' is the second book in the 'For Every Season' series. We are having so much fun. Follow us on our journey through hors d'oeuvres, entrees, soups, stews and chowders, sides, desserts and, finally, the menu book. Stay with us.

Thanks, Linda

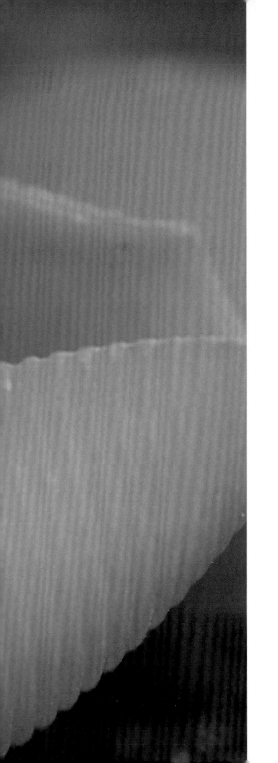

Summer

Autumn

Winter

Spring

Pasta

Cyclists at The Market in Malaga Cove Plaza after burning off last night's pasta carbs.

About Pasta

Pasta was first said to arrive in America courtesy of Marco Polo in the 13th century via China. Many others have laid claim to the invention of pasta. However, we know the ancient Romans prepared a dough of water and flour called lagane, later referred to as lasagne.

Pasta (which means "paste" in Italian) is simply semolina (durum wheat flour) combined with water or milk to create a dough that can be transformed into virtually hundreds of sizes, shapes, colors, and flavors. In fresh pasta, the liquid is replaced by eggs for a richer, more delicate flavor.

I discovered fresh pasta many years ago when I started flying to Italy. The authenticity and taste were new and amazing experiences for me. I couldn't believe so much passion could go into the actual mixing, rolling, and cutting of the pasta dough. What had always tasted somewhat heavy and filling became light, delicate, and unbelievably delicious. I wanted to experience this passionate process for myself. I practiced many, many recipes until I found a way to make it turn out well every time. Once you understand the feel and the texture of fresh pasta, the possibilities are endless.

Italians have pasta every day, and it must be cooked to perfection. Al dente (to the tooth) is critical. They use less sauce than Americans because the taste of the pasta itself is so important to their cooking. Quite honestly, pasta is an honored tradition.

It can be simple pasta for every day or a special pasta dish for holidays and celebrations. There are so many varieties available it isn't difficult to be creative when deciding upon a dish. It provides a perfect canvas for endless flavors and ingredients.

I never get tired of pasta. I eat it when I'm exhausted and want a quick meal to give me a lift. I eat it as comfort food, and I eat it when I want to celebrate. It is great on a cold night as a creamy lasagne, and light and refreshing on a summer day as a salad with fresh tomatoes and olive oil.

The recipes in this book are all my favorites. The ingredients are readily available and preparation is not difficult. There are many pasta shapes and thousands of ways to sauce them. Consult your own taste and style, and feel free to experiment. Take chances, because the truly best and only classical way to eat pasta is with great gusto.

- Always cook pasta in a pot that's big enough.

- Use a generous amount of water; the pasta should have plenty of room for the water to circulate around it.

- Salt the water. Be generous; it is really your only chance to season the pasta itself. And it will bring out the pasta's flavor.

- Never rinse cooked pasta; the starch adds more flavor and will help the sauce to adhere. The only exception is for cold salads. Rinse and add a little olive oil to keep it from sticking together.

- Save a ½ cup or so of pasta water to add to the sauce. It also adds flavor and will help the sauce to cling to the pasta.

A Note About Eggs

Ameraucana Chicken
"The Easter Egg Chicken"

The "Easter Egg Chicken" or Ameraucana chicken, originally came from Chile and was discovered by the Ameraucana Indians. They are bred to have eggs with shells of various pastel colors and designs. The hens have a distinctive full beard under their beak and produce a high number of colorful eggs, varying from pale to dark blue, with various shades of green and even pink.

Their meat is delicious, as are the eggs.

Fresh Eggs or Factory Farm Eggs?

Fresh: *Yolks have a neon orange color*
Factory Farm: *Yolks are the usual yellow*

There is a slight difference in texture, but a big difference in taste. Farm fresh eggs have a rich flavor that cannot be found in conventional farm eggs. The Italians use fresh eggs for their pasta. We are always asking ourselves as we sit in a trattoria or restaurant in Italy why their pasta is so much better than ours; fresh eggs- that's a big part of the answer. If you visit your local farmers market, you should find that the eggs have been collected that morning. Get some and try making pasta from scratch.

Fresh Egg Test and Storage

1. Fill a deep bowl with enough cold water to cover an egg. Put it in the water.
2. If your egg lies on its side on the bottom of the bowl, the air cell within is small and it's very fresh.
3. If the egg stands up and bobs on the bottom, the air cell is larger and the egg isn't quite as fresh.
4. If the egg floats on the surface, discard it.
5. Always store eggs in their original carton inside the refrigerator, not in the door.
6. Use within 2 weeks.

A Basic Pasta Dough

Makes 1 ½ Pounds Dough

2 ½ cups all-purpose flour
1 tablespoon olive oil
1 teaspoon salt
2 egg yolks
½ cup water

Preparing the Pasta Dough by Hand
- The pasta dough can be made entirely by hand.
- Place dry ingredients on a wooden board and make a well in the center.
- Mix liquid ingredients together. Pour into the well.
- With a fork gradually add the flour to the liquid until all of the flour is incorporated. Knead 3 or 4 times until the dough is smooth.
- Place the dough under a bowl to keep it moist until ready to roll out.

Preparing Pasta Dough In The Processor
- Combine flour and salt in bowl of processor. Turn machine quickly on and off, twice.
- Combine eggs, water and olive oil in a separate bowl. Turn on machine and add in a steady stream. Mixture should form a soft ball of dough, but not a sticky one. If it is too sticky, add one teaspoon of flour at a time while mixing until the dough is well formed. Slowly add drops of warm water to soften dough, if necessary.

To knead, allow ball of dough to process about 40 seconds, or until it is smooth and elastic.

- Turn out on lightly floured pastry board and knead briefly.
- Cover and allow the dough to rest for about 30 minutes.

To Shape Noodles With A Pasta Machine
- Divide dough into 3 equal portions. Working with 1 portion at a time, feed dough through the smooth rollers of the machine on setting #1. If using the machine to knead the dough, fold into thirds and repeat feeding dough through the rollers until smooth. Whenever the dough appears moist or sticky, lightly flour it.
- Set machine rollers closer together and feed dough through again, continuing through setting #6. Cut length of dough in half, if needed, so it is easier to handle.
- Cut the final strip into 10-12 inch lengths, or as desired. Feed dough through the blades of the cutting section.
- Place dough on floured wax paper and let dry, or hang on a pasta rack, for about 30 minutes before cooking.

Variations

The same recipe can be used to make different colored pasta and to incorporate different flavors:

- Spinach Pasta: Add ½ cup fresh spinach, wilted and squeezed dry, to the flour, salt and olive oil. Use only 1 egg.
- Tomato Pasta: Add 2 tablespoons tomato paste to the flour, salt and olive oil. Use 2 eggs. Add one to the flour, beat the second in a measuring cup, and pour half of it into the flour mixture.
- Basil Pasta: To the basic recipe add 3 tablespoons of a simple pesto.
- Black Pepper Pasta: To the basic recipe add 1 teaspoon freshly ground black pepper.
- Parmesan Pasta: To the basic recipe add ¼ cup grated Parmesan cheese.

Capelli d'angelo (Angel Hair)
Long, very thin spaghetti. It pairs best with a light sauce, so as not to weigh it down. Angel hair is great with olive oil, garlic, lemon and caviar. A simple, fresh tomato-basil sauce is delicious as well.

Maccheroni e Conchiglie (Elbows & Shells)
There is a wide variety of short, curved, tubular pasta sizes. These are classic for mac & cheese dishes. They are also very good in soups.

Fettuccine
'Fettuccine' is Italian for 'ribbons.' A little thicker and wider than linguine, it is most often served with cream sauces as in fettuccine alfredo.

Fusilli
The word comes from Italian referring to spiral of a rifle barrel; it literally means 'twisted spaghetti.' Can be topped with any sauce, added to soup or is beautiful in a salad.

Lasagne
Long, broad noodles with straight edges. Most commonly used to make lasagne with meat sauces, bechamel sauce and mozzarella.

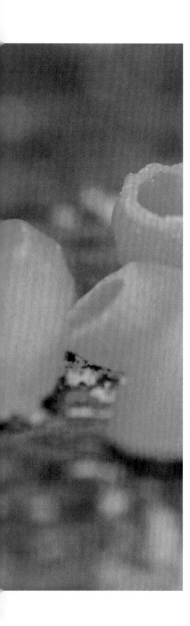

Linguine

Long flat pasta strands that are nice for sturdier sauces. Great with shellfish or mushrooms and truffle oil.

Orecchiette

This name translates to "little ears" from Italian. These tiny disk shapes are good with cream sauces that get into the 'ears'. Sometimes served with Italian sausage and broccoli rabe.

Orzo

A tiny, rice-shaped pasta that is good as a side dish with grilled vegetables or spinach. An outstanding entree with shrimp.

Pappardelle

Flat, long, wide noodles. This pasta shape stands up well to chicken, tomatoes, and olives tossed together.

Penne

Diagonally cut smooth tubes. Penne rigate have ridged sides. These small tubes are best used in soups, salads, or casseroles.

Ravioli

Square in shape and stuffed. Ravioli can be filled with vegetables, meats, fish, or cheese. Light sauces pair well served on top of the ravioli.

Rigatoni
A wide, ridged, tube-shaped pasta with holes on either end that can capture sauce inside. Super for baked dishes.

Spaghetti
Long, thin round strands. This classic is delicious with any sauce.

Tagliatelle
Long, thin, flat noodles about ¼ inch wide. Very similar to fettuccine and used with the same sauces.

Ziti
Relatively thin tubes that range in length. Memorable with hearty sauces and baked dishes.

This sauce freezes well. I always double or
triple the recipe so that I have it on hand.

Basic Marinara

3 tablespoons olive oil
1 cup finely chopped onions
1 tablespoon finely chopped garlic
4 cups Italian plum tomatoes, coarsely chopped
1 six-ounce can tomato paste
1 tablespoon dried oregano
1 tablespoon dried basil
1 bay leaf
2 teaspoons sugar
1 ½ teaspoons salt
Freshly ground black pepper

1. In a 3-4 quart saucepan, heat olive oil, add onions, and cook over medium heat for 7-8 minutes. When the onions are soft and transparent, add garlic and cook 1-2 minutes more.

2. Stir in tomatoes with their liquid, tomato paste, oregano, basil, bay leaf, sugar, salt and black pepper.

3. Bring the sauce to a boil, then turn heat very low and simmer uncovered for about 45 minutes.

4. When finished, the sauce should be thick and fairly smooth. Remove the bay leaf. Taste and season with salt and pepper.

5. For a smoother sauce, puree in the food processor after cooking.

Gaetano Giuliano, summer of 1928 in his neighborhood Italian grocery store in Melrose, Massachusetts, north of Boston. Pasta wasn't imported into the U.S. until the 1980's. Gaetano's store carried 10 to 12 varieties of pasta, the flat pastas home-made, the more complicated shapes bought in bulk from purveyors. The Giuliano Family emigrated from Sicily to the Boston area, and finally to Southern California where they are known today for their quality pasta and famous Italian dishes.

Arrabiata Sauce

¼ cup olive oil
3 cloves garlic, thinly sliced
2 teaspoons red pepper flakes
½ cup sliced kalamata olives
3 tablespoons drained capers
1 28-ounce can Italian tomatoes, chopped
¼ cup chopped Italian parsley
Salt to taste

- Heat olive oil in a skillet over moderate heat. Add garlic and red pepper flakes. As soon as the flakes begin to color the oil and the garlic is golden, drain the tomatoes and coarsely chop. Add the oil and red pepper flakes. Stir in olives and capers. Cook for about 10 minutes.

  Quick Dinner: This goes well over some cooked penne, with additional parsley and freshly grated Parmesan cheese.

Bechamel Sauce

4 tablespoons butter
4 tablespoons flour
2 cups milk
½ cup heavy cream
Freshly ground black pepper

• Melt butter in a saucepan. Add flour and stir until the roux is frothy and the taste of raw flour is gone. Meanwhile, heat milk in another pan. Add the warmed milk gradually to the roux, stirring continuously. Turn up the heat and cook, stirring, until the sauce is almost boiling. Turn down the heat and let simmer for a few minutes. Stir in heavy cream and pepper.

Quick Dinner: Béchamel forms the base of the best Mac & Cheese on Earth: add 8 ounces grated Cheddar cheese, 1 teaspoon hot sauce and ½ pound cooked macaroni. Put into a baking dish, top with additional cheese and bake for 30 minutes at 350 degrees.

Brown Butter-Pine Nut Sauce

½ cup pine nuts
8 tablespoons butter
Salt and pepper
¼ cup chopped Italian parsley

- Heat a small saucepan and toast pine nuts until golden, about 5 minutes. Set aside. Melt the butter in medium skillet. Cook, swirling the pan, until the butter turns golden brown, about 5 minutes. Stir in the reserved nuts, salt and parsley.

Quick Dinner: Delicious on butternut squash ravioli.

Gorgonzola Sauce

2 tablespoons butter
3 shallots, finely chopped
1 tablespoon plus 2 teaspoons chopped fresh thyme
2 cups heavy cream
½ pound gorgonzola cheese, crumbled
Freshly ground black pepper

- Melt butter in a heavy skillet over medium heat. Add shallots and sauté until translucent, about 5 minutes. Stir in the tablespoon of thyme. Add cream and Gorgonzola, and stir until cheese melts and sauce thickens slightly. Season with pepper.

Quick Dinner: Serve with fettuccine and toasted walnuts or gnocchi, and additional thyme.

Marinara Sauce

3 tablespoons olive oil
1 cup finely chopped onions
1 tablespoon finely sliced garlic
4 cups Italian plum tomatoes, coarsely chopped
4 tablespoons tomato paste (from tube)
1 tablespoon dried oregano
¼ teaspoon red pepper flakes
2 teaspoons sugar
1 ½ teaspoons salt
Freshly ground black pepper

- In a 3-4 quart saucepan, heat olive oil and cook onions over moderate heat for 5 minutes.
- When onions turn soft, add the garlic for 2 more minutes. Stir in tomatoes and their liquid, tomato paste, oregano, red pepper flakes, and sugar. Simmer for a few minutes and season with more salt and pepper to taste.

Quick Dinner: This goes well with most pasta, especially spaghetti or linguine.

Arugula Pesto

2 cloves garlic
2 cups fresh arugula
½ teaspoon red pepper flakes

½ cup olive oil
½ cup freshly grated Parmesan cheese
Salt and pepper

- Place garlic in the bowl of a food processor. When finely chopped, add arugula and red pepper flakes to combine. Gradually add olive oil and then Parmesan cheese. Season to taste with salt and pepper.

Quick Dinner: Serve with spaghetti and tomatoes roasted under the broiler.

Basil Pesto

2 tablespoons pine nuts
2 cloves garlic
½ teaspoon salt
½ teaspoon red pepper flakes
2 cups packed basil leaves
½ cup olive oil
3 tablespoons Parmesan cheese
¼ cup heavy cream

- Pulse pine nuts and salt together in a food processor until finely ground. Add garlic and basil and, with the motor running, drizzle in the olive oil. Add Parmesan cheese. Warm the pesto in a large skillet and add cream.

Quick Dinner: Combine the sauce with cooked gnocchi. Stir together and serve with additional cheese on the side.

Sun-Dried Tomato Pesto

¾ cup plump moist sun-dried tomatoes
2 cloves garlic
½ teaspoon red pepper flakes
¼ cup olive oil
Salt

- In a food processor, process sun-dried tomatoes with garlic, red pepper flakes, and olive oil until mixture is smooth.

  Quick Dinner: Toss with spaghettini and sprinkle with chopped arugula and Parmesan cheese.

Vodka Sauce

5 tablespoons butter
⅔ cup vodka
½ teaspoon red pepper flakes
1 can Italian plum tomatoes, drained and pureed
¾ cup heavy cream
½ teaspoon salt

- Melt butter in a large skillet over medium heat. Add vodka and red pepper flakes, then simmer for 2 minutes. Add the pureed tomatoes and cream and simmer for 5 minutes longer. Season with salt.

  Quick Dinner: Toss with cooked penne, ¾ cup Parmesan cheese and ¼ cup finely chopped parsley.

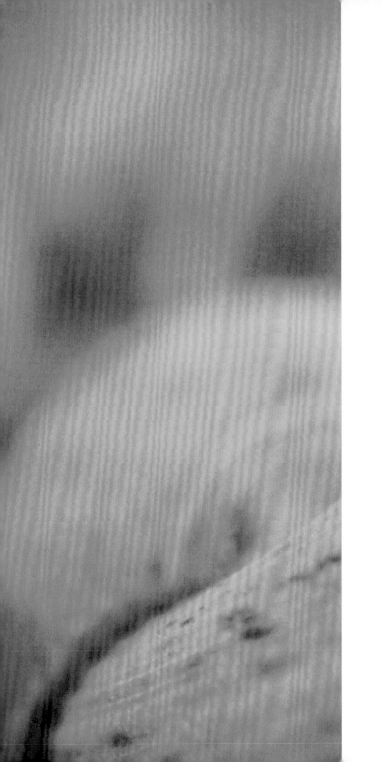

Summer

Fettuccine with Grilled Lobster Tails

Serves 6

Two 1-pound lobster tails cut in half
½ cup fresh mint leaves
½ cup fresh basil leaves
1 cup parsley leaves
2 garlic cloves
¼ cup capers, rinsed well and drained
4 medium plum tomatoes, chopped
1 teaspoon red pepper flakes
1 teaspon freshly ground black pepper
½ cup olive oil
1 pound fettuccine

1. Bring a large pot of water to a boil and add a generous amount of salt.

2. Cut the lobster tails down the middle and coat with olive oil. Preheat the grill to high. Place the tails on the grill shell side down for 3 minutes. Turn and cook for another 3 minutes. Leave in the shell or remove and cut into large chunks.

3. In a food processor, puree the mint, basil, parsley, garlic, capers, tomatoes, red pepper flakes, black pepper and olive oil to form a smooth paste. If needed, add a little more oil. Combine this with the lobster meat if you have cut it into chunks. If not, serve the split lobster tails on top of the pasta. Cook the fettuccine for about 10 minutes, until tender but still al dente, and drain well. Add the pasta to the bowl with lobster and pesto until well mixed. Serve immediately.

This pasta is great with the grilled lobster, but grilled shrimp or scallops are also good.

Spaghettini with Spicy Greens & Parmesan

Serves 4-6

½ cup pine nuts
⅓ cup olive oil
6 cloves garlic, minced
¾ teaspoon dried red pepper flakes
¾ pound mixed greens, such as mustard greens, collard, spinach or broccoli rabe, cut into 1 ½-inch pieces
¾ teaspoon salt
2 cups chicken stock
1 pound spaghettini
1 ½ cups grated Parmesan cheese, plus more for serving

1. In a small frying pan, toast the pine nuts over medium heat, stirring frequently, until they are golden brown.

2. In a large pan, heat olive oil over medium-low heat. Add garlic and red pepper flakes, and cook until the garlic is soft but not brown, about 1 minute. Increase heat to high, add greens and salt then let cook, stirring, until greens wilt, 1-2 minutes. Add chicken stock, bring to a simmer and cook 5 minutes longer.

3. In a large pot of boiling water, cook the spaghettini until just done, about 10 minutes. Drain. Toss with mixed greens and stock. Add Parmesan and pine nuts, toss again and serve.

Instead of adding the chicken to the pasta,
I like to slice it and fan it on the plate. It's
a nice presentation with some chives.

Grilled Chicken Spaghetti with Spinach & Candied Tomatoes

Serves 6

¼ cup pine nuts
1 pound boneless, skinless chicken breast, grilled and then thinly sliced
1 tablespoon garlic, thinly sliced
¼ cup white wine
½ cup chicken broth
¾ pound spaghetti
1 bag fresh spinach
4 ounces soft goat cheese, crumbled
¾ pound cherry tomatoes
¼ cup sugar
¼ cup sherry vinegar

1. Bring a large pot of salted water to a boil for the spaghetti and spinach.

2. Toast pine nuts in a large sauté pan over medium heat until golden, tossing often for 3 minutes. Transfer to a plate and season with salt. Return pan to the burner.

3. Brush chicken breasts with olive oil and grill for 4 minutes on each side. Slice thinly and set aside. In a skillet, sauté garlic for 30 seconds. Deglaze the pan with white wine, and add broth. Boil for 1 minute; add grilled chicken and set aside.

4. Cook the spaghetti according to package directions. Just before draining, add spinach, cook 30 seconds, then drain, reserving ½ cup of the water. Toss pasta and spinach with goat cheese and chicken mixture in a large bowl; thin with pasta water, if necessary. Keep warm.

5. Sauté tomatoes in 1 tablespoon oil for 2 minutes over high heat in the pan used for the chicken. Add sugar and vinegar; simmer until syrupy, 2-3 minutes. Season with salt.

6. Garnish pasta with tomatoes and pine nuts.

Pappardelle with Zucchini, Anchovies and Mint

Serves 6

2 ounces anchovies, drained and minced
¼ cup finely chopped mint
2 tablespoons snipped chives
¼ cup plus 2 tablespoons olive oil
4 large garlic cloves, thinly sliced
¼ teaspoon crushed red pepper
1 ½ pounds medium zucchini,
thinly sliced lengthwise (vegetable peeler
works well)
Coarse sea salt
1 pound pappardelle
Freshly grated Parmesan cheese
Lemon wedges, for serving

1. In a large bowl, mix the anchovies, mint, chives and 2 tablespoons of the oil.

2. In a large skillet, reheat the remaining 1/4 cup oil until shimmering. Add the garlic and crushed red pepper; cook over moderate heat until the garlic is lightly golden, about 3 minutes.

3. Add the zucchini, season with salt and cook over moderately high heat, tossing, until crisp tender, about 5 minutes.

4. Meanwhile, cook the pappardelle in a large pot of boiling salted water until al dente.

5. Drain, reserving 1/2 cup of the pasta water. Return the pasta to the pot. Add the zucchini and the reserved pasta water and toss over moderate heat.

6. Transfer the pasta to the bowl with the anchovies and herbs, season with salt and toss well.

7. Serve right away, passing the Parmesan and lemon wedges at the table.

I know, anchovies (Ugh!!). Try this combination with the mint. It works!

Risotto with Tomato & Basil

Serves 6

1 ½ pounds fresh plum tomatoes
6 cups chicken broth
1 tablespoon olive oil
2 tablespoons butter
⅓ cup chopped shallots
2 cloves garlic, finely chopped
¼ teaspoon red pepper flakes
Salt and freshly ground pepper
2 cups Arborio rice
¾ cup grated Parmesan cheese
Fresh basil leaves

This summer risotto is best with tomatoes at their peak. Simple and delicious!

1. Peel and seed the tomatoes. Cut the tomatoes in half lengthwise and julienne.

2. Heat broth to a simmer in a saucepan.

3. Heat oil and butter in a skillet, add shallots and garlic; cook until golden.

4. Add tomatoes, red pepper flakes, salt and pepper. Cook together for about 10 minutes.

5. Add rice and mix thoroughly, making sure rice is well covered with the hot sauce.

6. Add 1 cup of broth at a time to the rice and stir continuously until all of the liquid is absorbed. Continue adding the broth, stirring constantly until the rice is al dente, for about 20 minutes.

7. Add the cheese and torn basil. Stir and serve.

Fettuccine with Smoky
Bacon & Caramelized Corn

Serves 6

1 pound fettuccine
1 tablespoon olive oil
3 ounces thickly sliced applewood smoked
bacon, cut into ½-inch dice
1 medium onion, finely chopped
½ teaspoon minced garlic
3 cups fresh white corn kernels
½ cup chicken stock
1 ½ cups heavy cream
1 teaspoon minced fresh thyme
Salt and freshly ground pepper
2 large plum tomatoes, seeded and
finely diced
1 teaspoon balsamic vinegar
Scallion greens, cut lengthwise into very
fine julienne

1. Heat 1 ½ teaspoons of oil in a large skil-
    let. Add bacon and cook over medium
    heat until most of the fat is rendered,
    about 5 minutes. Add onion and garlic,
    and stir to cook until translucent, about
    4 minutes.

2. Add corn, reserving ⅓ cup, to skillet and
    cook over moderately high heat, stir-
    ring, until the corn is browned, about 4
    minutes. Add chicken stock and bring
    to a boil. Add cream and boil, stirring,
    until reduced by a third, 3-5 minutes.
    Add thyme and season well with salt and
    pepper.

3. Heat the remaining 1 ½ teaspoons oil
    in a nonreactive skillet. Add reserved ⅓
    cup corn and sauté over medium heat
    until toasted, about 3 minutes. Add
    tomatoes and vinegar; season with salt
    and pepper. Stir to cook until the toma-
    toes are just soft, about 2 minutes.

4. Cook pasta in a large pot of boiling
    water until al dente. Drain and transfer
    to a bowl; toss with the creamed corn
    sauce. Garnish with toasted corn and
    julienned scallions to serve.

Place the scallion greens in a bowl of ice water. They'll be crisp with a vibrant green color.

Arugula, Sun-Dried Tomatoes & Orzo

Serves 6

1 ½ cups orzo
⅓ cup oil-packed, chopped, drained, sun-dried tomatoes
5 tablespoons olive oil
¼ cup balsamic vinegar
¼ cup packed chopped kalamata olives
1 cup chopped arugula
½ cup pine nuts, toasted
½ cup chopped fresh basil
½ cup freshly grated Parmesan cheese
2 large garlic cloves, minced

1. Cook orzo in a pot of boiling, salted water until tender to the bite, about 8 to 10 minutes. Drain well. Transfer to a large bowl.

2. Add sun-dried tomatoes, oil, vinegar and olives; toss to blend.

3. Mix chopped arugula, pine nuts, chopped basil, Parmesan and garlic into orzo mixture. Season to taste with salt and pepper to serve.

This pasta can be served slightly warm or at room temperature with grilled chicken or beef.

Serves 10

Spicy Tomato Sauce
¼ cup olive oil
1 medium onion, finely chopped
6 garlic cloves, minced
Two 28-ounce cans roma tomatoes, broken
into pieces, with their juice
1 cup tightly-packed, pitted kalamata olives,
coarsely chopped
2 tablespoons tomato paste
2 tablespoons drained capers
2 tablespoons minced
anchovy fillets (about 8)
½ teaspoon dried basil
½ teaspoon crushed red pepper
Salt to taste

Pesto Oil
2 cloves garlic, minced
½ teaspoon red pepper flakes
2 cups loosely packed basil leaves
1 cup olive oil
1 teaspoon salt, or to taste

Grilled Vegetables
4 medium zucchini, cut lengthwise into
¼-inch slices

4 red or yellow bell peppers, roasted,
seeded and peeled, cut into large pieces
2 medium eggplants, cut into
¼-inch rounds
2 large yellow onions, cut
into ¼-inch rounds
¼ cup olive oil
1 tablespoon salt

2 pounds ricotta cheese
1 ¼ pounds uncooked dried
lasagna noodles
2 cups grated mozzarella cheese

1. Make the Spicy Tomato Sauce: Heat
    olive oil in a large pot over medium-high
    heat. Add onion and cook until soft and
    slightly caramelized, about 6 minutes.
    Add garlic and cook for 2 minutes, stir-
    ring frequently. Add tomatoes and the
    remaining ingredients; simmer until the
    sauce has thickened and slightly reduces,
    about 40 minutes. Adjust seasoning to
    taste, cover and set aside.

2. Make the Pesto Oil: Combine garlic and

Grilled Vegetable Lasagne with Spicy Tomato-Olive Sauce & Pesto Oil

basil in the bowl of a food processor or blender and process on high while adding olive oil in a steady stream. Continue to process until well blended, season with salt to taste, and set aside until ready to assemble the lasagne.

3. Grill the vegetables: Preheat a grill or broiler. In a large, shallow bowl, toss the zucchini, bell peppers, eggplant and onions with olive oil and salt. Grill or broil in batches, turning the vegetables once, until they are tender, lightly browned and have released most of their moisture, 5 to 6 minutes per side.

4. Preheat oven to 350 degrees and lightly grease a 9x13-inch baking dish.

5. Combine ricotta cheese with ½ cup Pesto Oil in medium bowl and set aside.

6. Spoon ½ cup of the spicy tomato sauce onto the bottom of the prepared baking dish. Cover with a single layer of lasagne noodles, making sure they do not overlap. Top the lasagne with a layer of ricotta cheese, then a layer of grilled vegetables, a layer of grated mozzarella and sauce until all the ingredients have been used, ending with mozzarella.

7. Cover the lasagne with aluminum foil and bake for 45 minutes. Remove foil and continue to bake until the lasagne is bubbling and golden brown, 15 to 30 minutes longer. Let rest for 10 minutes before serving; drizzle with some of the remaining Pesto Oil.

Pesto Pizza

1 ball store-bought pizza dough, brought
to room temperature and rested
for an hour
2 cloves garlic, lightly crushed
½ teaspoon red pepper flakes
2 cups fresh basil
½ cup olive oil
2 tablespoons pine nuts
1 teaspoon salt

8 sliced plum tomatoes
½ cup freshly grated Parmesan cheese

1. Put the garlic, red pepper flakes, basil, olive oil, pine nuts, tomatoes and salt in the food processor. Add grated cheese by hand. Pesto topping can be prepared ahead and stored, covered, in the refrigerator for up to 2 days.

2. Place a pizza stone on the lowest rack of the oven. Preheat to 500 degrees.

3. Divide pizza dough into 2 large pizzas or 6 small ones. By hand, stretch one piece into a round. Alternatively, with a rolling pin, roll out on a lightly floured surface. (Keep remaining dough covered with a towel or plastic wrap to retain moisture while working.) Place the round on a cornmeal-dusted pizza peel using enough cornmeal so that the dough slides easily.

4. Spread 1 tablespoon pesto on each round of dough. Arrange ½ cup sliced tomatoes over top of each one. Season lightly with salt and pepper.

5. Carefully slide the pizza from the peel onto the heated pizza stone.

6. Bake for 10 to 15 minutes, or until the bottoms are crisp and browned.

Linda's Linguine with White Clam Sauce

Serves 6

3 pounds fresh clams
Fresh-grated pepper
¼ cup olive oil
6 cloves garlic, smashed
1 teaspoon red pepper flakes
Zest and juice of 1 lemon
1 cup dry white wine
½ cup water
1 pound imported linguine
2 tablespoons butter
3 tablespoons chopped Italian parsley
2 tablespoons chopped oregano
1 cup Parmesan
Salt
Olive oil for drizzling

1. Place clams in very cold water to soak. Add a few grinds of pepper to remove any dirt from the shells. Soak for 30 minutes. Lift them out of the water a few at a time, rinse under cold running water and place in a bowl.

2. Heat olive oil in a large skillet. Add garlic, red pepper flakes, zest and lemon juice. Add clams, dry white wine and water. Cover skillet and turn to high heat. Shake pan gently back and forth every couple of minutes. Check the clams after 5 minutes; when done, the shells will open. Be careful not to overcook.

3. Boil pasta until al dente.

4. Quickly remove clams from the skillet. Add cooked pasta with butter, parsley and oregano so that the pasta mixes with and absorbs the flavorful clam juices. Place pasta into a serving boil, allowing the juice in the bottom of the pan to drain on top. Arrange the cooked clams in their shells on top of the pasta. Sprinkle with the Parmesan cheese and a drizzle of olive oil.

I know it is not traditionally Italian to add Parmesan cheese to seafood,
but I love the salty flavor it adds to the clams.

This fettuccine is great with grilled salmon on top.

Spinach Fettuccine

Serves 6

1 pound fettuccine noodles
4 cups fresh baby spinach
½ teaspoon red pepper flakes
½ cup shredded Parmesan cheese
2 tablespoons olive oil
Salt and pepper to taste

1. Bring a pot of salted water to a boil for the fettuccine. Cook the pasta for about 10 minutes until al dente.

2. Place spinach, red pepper flakes, Parmesan and olive oil in a large bowl. Drain pasta, add to the bowl and toss to coat and wilt spinach. Season with salt and pepper.

Frittata Di Pasta with Sun-Dried Tomatoes

Serves 6

Salt
8 ounces dried spaghetti, or leftover
cooked pasta
½ cup drained oil-packed sun-dried
tomatoes, chopped
4 large eggs
¾ cup freshly grated Parmesan cheese
¾ cup freshly grated fontina cheese
1 clove garlic, grated
½ teaspoon red pepper flakes
1 ½ teaspoons salt
½ teaspoon freshly ground black pepper
1 tablespoon unsalted butter
1 tablespoon olive oil

1. If using dried pasta, bring a large pot of salted water to a boil. Add the spaghetti and cook, stirring occasionally, until tender but still firm to the bite, about 8 minutes. Drain.

2. In a large bowl, toss the spaghetti with sun-dried tomatoes, then set aside to cool.

3. In a medium bowl, whisk eggs, Parmesan, fontina, garlic, red pepper flakes, salt and pepper to blend. Add egg mixture to the cooled spaghetti mixture, and toss to coat.

4. Preheat the broiler. In a 10-inch oven-proof non-stick skillet, melt butter over medium heat. Transfer spaghetti mixture to the skillet, pressing to form an even layer. Cook until the bottom is golden brown, about 3 minutes. Transfer skillet to the oven and broil until the top is golden brown, about 5 minutes. Let the frittata cool to room temperature, and then invert onto a platter.

5. Cut into wedges and serve at room temperature.

This pasta dish is delicious for brunch or lunch. Any left over grilled vegetables would be great to use as well.

Autumn

Gratin of Shells with Tiger Prawns & Spinach

Serves 8

18 pieces of extra-large shell pasta
2 tablespoons olive oil
1 cup chopped bacon
5 large shallots, minced
1 clove garlic, minced
1 ½ tablespoons all-purpose flour
1 cup white wine
2 cups cream
1 cup grated Fontina
½ cup grated sharp Cheddar
2 tablespoons grated Parmesan
18 large Tiger shrimp, peeled and deveined
2 cups gently packed spinach
Salt and ground pepper
Hot pepper sauce (Crystal)
½ cup bread crumbs
¼ cup chopped Italian parsley leaves

1. Preheat the broiler.

2. Bring a large pot of water to a rolling boil, add pasta shells and cook al dente for about 10 minutes.

3. Meanwhile in a large skillet, add olive oil and bacon, cooking until just crisp, then add shallots and garlic. Cook and stir over moderate heat just until shallots are translucent. Add flour, stirring to cook constantly to blend and toast the flour, about 5 minutes. Add white wine, and reduce until almost dry. Add cream, bring to a simmer until the sauce coats the back of a spoon, about 5 to 10 minutes. Remove from heat and stir in the cheeses, shrimp and spinach. Keep gently stirring until cheese melts, spinach wilts and shrimp begins to turn pink. Season with salt and pepper to taste, adding hot sauce if desired.

4. Drain the pasta well, getting out excess moisture from the shells.

5. In a large ovenproof baking dish, place drained shells. Put a shrimp in each with cheese mixture. Sprinkle with breadcrumbs and chopped parsley. Place under broiler until the breadcrumbs are toasted, about 2 to 3 minutes.

This makes a great do-ahead pasta for a crowd.
Serve with a salad and grilled garlic bread.

Linguine with Applewood-Smoked Bacon, Butter, Pecorino, Arugula & Black Pepper

Serves 6

Salt
1 cup arugula, cut into julienne strips
1 pound linquine
4 tablespoons butter, room temperature
1 ¼ cups very finely grated
Pecorino Romano
1 ½ teaspoons freshly ground black pepper
6 slices cooked applewood-smoked
bacon, chopped

1. Bring a large pot of salted water to a boil over high heat. Add linguine and cook until al dente, stirring frequently for about 8 minutes. Drain, reserving 1 cup of the pasta water.

2. Immediately toss the hot pasta in a large bowl with butter to coat. While tossing, gradually sprinkle cheese, pepper, and enough of the reserved pasta water evenly over the linguine to moisten. Add arugula and toss to combine. Season the pasta to taste with salt. Divide the pasta among plates with bacon and serve.

Tortellini in Asparagus-Gorgonzola Sauce

Serves 6

1 pound cheese tortellini
1 pound asparagus, ends trimmed,
cut into 1-inch pieces
6 tablespoons unsalted butter
2 large shallots, finely chopped
1 ½ cups heavy cream
¼ pound crumbled Gorgonzola cheese
¼ cup grated Pecorino cheese
Freshly ground black pepper
½ cup chopped fresh Italian parsley

1. In a large saucepan, bring 4 quarts of water to a boil. Add salt and boil tortellini for about 8 to 10 minutes. Lift tortellini from the water and add asparagus for about 3 minutes.

2. While the pasta and asparagus are cooking, heat butter in a medium saucepan. Add shallots and cook for 1 minute. Stir in cream, cheeses and pepper. Cook the sauce for 3 to 4 minutes until cheese is melted and sauce has thickened slightly. Stir in tortellini and asparagus, and cook just until warmed through.

3. Place on a serving platter and sprinkle with parsley.

This simple pasta is great as a first course or a side with grilled pork or chicken.

I cheat sometimes and buy premade spinach ravioli. The sauce is always good.

Spinach-Stuffed Ravioli with
Red Pepper-Basil Sauce

Serves 6

1 recipe pasta dough
6 ounces goat cheese
1 cup ricotta cheese
1 10-ounce package frozen chopped
spinach, defrosted, placed in a towel to
remove water
¼ cup minced fresh herbs (Italian parsley,
basil, rosemary)
Salt and freshly ground pepper

Sauce
4 large cloves garlic, minced
1 cup finely chopped onion
1 teaspoon red pepper flakes, or 1 whole
dried red pepper
½ teaspoon dried thyme, crumbled
2 tablespoons olive oil
4 red bell peppers, sliced thin
1 cup chicken broth
2 tablespoons butter
4 tablespoons finely chopped
fresh basil leaves
Fresh lemon juice to taste
Parmesan cheese

1. Combine filling ingredients in a small bowl or in the food processor.

2. Divide the pasta dough into four pieces. Roll out dough to the number six setting on pasta machine. Fill pasta with spinach mixture and cut into rounds or squares.

3. Bring large pot of water to a rapid boil.

4. Prepare the sauce: In a small skillet cook garlic, onion, red pepper flakes, thyme, salt and pepper to taste in the oil over moderately low heat, stirring, until the onion is softened; add bell peppers and broth. Simmer, covered, for 10 minutes, or until the peppers are very soft. In a blender or food processor, puree the mixture until smooth. Return to skillet and swirl in the butter. Stir in basil, lemon juice, more salt and pepper to taste. Keep sauce warm.

5. Cook ravioli until al dente in boiling water. Drain and transfer to a serving bowl.

6. Add sauce, toss and serve with Parmesan.

The balsamic tomatoes are great on sandwiches or as part of an antipasti platter.

Spaghettini with Arugula & Roasted Balsamic Tomatoes

Serves 6

Roasted Balsamic Tomatoes
9 ripe plum tomatoes
4 tablespoons olive oil
4 tablespoons balsamic vinegar
Salt and pepper

1. Preheat oven to 450 degrees. Cut tomatoes in half lengthwise and place on a roasting pan, cut side up. Drizzle with olive oil and balsamic vinegar. Salt and pepper lightly. Place in the oven for 20 minutes. Remove and cool to room temperature.

Spaghettini
1 pound dried spaghettini
6 tablespoons pesto
2 tablespoons olive oil, plus more for serving
5 ounces pecorino cheese
2 bunches of arugula
4 tablespoons balsamic vinegar
Salt and pepper
18 balsamic roasted tomato halves

1. Add a little olive oil to the pesto to thin, and reserve.

2. Shave 12 slices from the block of pecorino cheese. Grate the remainder.

3. Dress arugula with the balsamic vinegar and reserve.

4. Cook spaghettini in a large pot of boiling water until al dente. Drain and transfer to a large bowl while still slightly wet.

5. Toss the spaghettini with pesto oil until coated evenly, then add arugula and grated cheese. Gently toss and season to taste.

6. Put three tomato halves on each plate and mound the spaghetti mixture on top. Top each with shavings of cheese and drizzle with a little more oil. Finish with ground pepper if desired.

Fettuccine with Creamy Piquillo Pepper-Feta Sauce

Serves 6

2 tablespoons olive oil
1 shallot, chopped
3 cloves garlic, thinly sliced
1 teaspoon red pepper flakes
1 15-ounce jar piquillo peppers,
drained and chopped
½ cup chicken stock
1 cup crumbled feta cheese
1 pound fettuccine
Salt and freshly ground black pepper
2 tablespoons chopped fresh parsley

1. Heat oil in heavy skillet over medium heat. Sauté shallot, garlic and red pepper flakes until soft. Add peppers and sauté until heated through. Remove from heat and let cool slightly.

2. Place pepper mixture in bowl of a food processor with chicken stock and all but 2 tablespoons of feta cheese. Process until smooth.

3. Cook pasta until al dente. Drain, reserving ½ cup of the pasta water. Toss pasta with sauce, adding pasta water to thin if needed. Season with salt and pepper to taste.

4. Sprinkle with parsley and remaining cheese.

Piquillo peppers are readily available and are very sweet. They pair well with the feta cheese and red pepper flakes.

Tiger Prawns & Spicy Roasted Red Pepper Pasta

Serves 4-6

2 jalapeño chiles, roasted
1 ½ cups roasted, peeled and
seeded red peppers
Salt and freshly ground pepper
1 tablespoon roasted garlic
paste (if desired)
2 tablespoons olive oil
1 pound tiger prawns
1 ½ tablespoons minced garlic
1 tablespoon finely chopped fresh oregano
4 cups chicken stock
¾ pound dried orzo
2 tablespoons finely chopped flat-leaf
parsley
1 cup freshly grated Parmesan

1. Roast jalapeños and red peppers under the broiler until skins are charred and blackened. Place in a zip-lock plastic bag for 10 minutes, and then remove charred skins.

2. Place 1 jalapeño and the roasted peppers in a blender with salt and pepper to taste and puree until smooth. Taste and add the second jalapeño, if desired. The sauce should be noticeably spicy, as it will be flavoring all the pasta. Add garlic paste, if using. Sauce should amount to 1 ¼ cups; set aside.

3. Heat 1 tablespoon olive oil in a large sauté pan over medium-high heat until hot. Add prawns and spread evenly so they do not boil . Season well with salt and pepper. Continue to sauté for about 3 minutes, until they are just cooked through and have turned pink. Remove to a plate with a slotted spoon. Discard any liquid left in pan.

4. Add remaining 1 tablespoon olive oil to

the pan and heat over medium-high heat until hot. Add garlic and sauté briefly until light brown. Stir in oregano. Add chicken stock and bring to a boil. Add the pasta with salt and pepper to taste. Reduce heat to medium-low and simmer slowly, stirring occasionally so the pasta does not stick for about 12 minutes.

5. When the pasta is ready, stir in the pepper puree. Return shrimp to the pan until heated through. Add parsley and all but 1 tablespoon of Parmesan. Stir again. Pour into a warm serving bowl and dust with the remaining tablespoon of cheese. Serve immediately.

Baked Lasagne with Asparagus & Pesto

Serves 6

Pesto Sauce
3 tablespoons pine nuts
2 cups basil leaves
1 clove garlic
Pinch of sea salt
¼ teaspoon red pepper flakes
½ cup grated Parmesan
3 tablespoons grated pecorino cheese
1 ¼ cups olive oil

Béchamel
5 tablespoons unsalted butter
¼ cup flour
3 cups milk
2 teaspoons salt
½ teaspoon freshly grated nutmeg

1 ½ pounds medium asparagus spears
Fresh or dried pasta sheets
2 cups bechamel
1 cup pesto sauce
1 cup grated Pecorino cheese
½ cup bread crumbs

Pesto
1. Place pine nuts, basil, garlic and sea salt in a food processor and process to a paste. Add pepper flakes and cheese, then drizzle in olive oil. Store in a jar, topped with foil. Makes 2 ½ cups.

Béchamel
1. In a medium saucepan, heat butter until melted. Add flour and whisk until smooth. Cook over medium heat until light golden brown, about 6 minutes. Add milk to the butter mixture, whisking continuously until very smooth, and bring to a boil. Season with salt and nutmeg.

Perhaps the best invention in Italian cooking, "No-boil" pasta sheets save time and sanity. They will cook in the sauce, cutting prep time significantly.

1. Preheat the oven to 400 degrees.

2. Trim asparagus and grill for about 5 minutes.. Cut each spear in half crosswise. Set aside.

3. In a mixing bowl, stir béchamel, pesto and grated cheese together until mixed well. Butter individual gratin dishes and place 1 sheet of pasta on the bottom of each. Top each with 3 pieces of asparagus and 2 tablespoons of pesto, followed by another sheet of pasta. Continue with this layering until you have 4 of each layer. Lay one more sheet of pasta on top, followed by a spoonful of pesto mixture and sprinkle with bread crumbs. Place dishes on a baking sheet and bake for 20 to 25 minutes, or until bubbling and golden brown on top. Serve immediately.

Gnocchi with Asparagus & Pancetta

Serves 6

2 packages vacuum-packed gnocchi
4 ounces pancetta, cut into thin strips
¼ cup thinly sliced shallots
1 ½ pounds asparagus, trimmed and cut
into 1 ½-inch pieces
3 cloves garlic, thinly sliced
2 tablespoons lemon juice
¼ teaspoon salt
¼ teaspoon red pepper flakes
Freshly grated pepper
½ cup shaved Parmesan cheese

1. Cook gnocchi according to package directions. Drain in a colander over a bowl, reserving ½ cup cooking liquid. Keep warm.

2. Heat a large nonstick skillet over medium-high heat. Add pancetta; sauté 3 minutes or until lightly browned. Transfer to a paper towel-lined plate.

3. Add shallots and asparagus to pan; sauté 5 minutes or until tender. Stir in garlic and sauté for 1 minute. Add gnocchi, pancetta, reserved cooking liquid, lemon juice, salt, pepper flakes and pepper to the pan. Cook until heated through.

4. Serve with shaved Parmesan cheese.

I love packages of vacuum-packed gnocchi. They are so fast and easy, and they are really good. Most markets carry them now.

Roasted Tomato Spaghetti with Kalamata Olives

Serves 6

3 tablespoons olive oil
1 cup chopped red onion
4 cloves garlic, minced
⅓ cup pitted kalamata olives
3 anchovy fillets, drained
½ teaspoon red pepper flakes
1 teaspoon dried oregano
1 (28-ounce) can San Marzano tomatoes, with juice, roughly chopped
Salt
Freshly ground pepper
1 pound spaghetti
3 tablespoons minced fresh parsley

1. Heat the oven to 450 degrees.

2. In a large cast-iron skillet, combine olive oil, onion, garlic, olives, anchovies, pepper flakes, and oregano. Place on low heat and bring to a simmer, stirring for 2 minutes. Remove from the heat and pour tomatoes over the top; season with salt and pepper.

3. Transfer to oven and roast for 20 minutes until sauce is hot and bubbly, and onions are soft.

4. Meanwhile, cook the spaghetti in boiling, salted water for about 10 minutes. Drain and add to the skillet with the sauce.

5. Drizzle with a little more olive oil and sprinkle with parsley. Serve the pasta from the cast-iron skillet with grilled ciabatta.

Spaghetti Puttanesca with Tomato, Olives & Capers

Serves 6

1 pound spaghetti, cooked in boiling salted water for about 10 minutes
6 tablespoons olive oil
4 garlic cloves, sliced
½ teaspoon red pepper flakes
3 canned anchovy fillets
1 (14 ½ ounce) can diced tomatoes, drained
2 tablespoons tomato paste
20 small pitted black Italian olives cut in half or kalamatas
3 tablespoons capers
½ cup fresh parsley, chopped
Salt and pepper to taste

1. In a large skillet combine olive oil, garlic, pepper flakes and anchovies. Cook for about 5 minutes, mashing the anchovies with a fork. Add tomatoes, tomato paste and olives and cook for an additional 10 minutes. Add capers.

2. Drain the pasta and pour into skillet. Stir well to mix. Sprinkle with parsley. Taste for salt and pepper, serve.

Pasta is often comfort food for me. This sauce is one of my favorites. The name puttanesca is a derivation of puttana, meaning "whore" in Italian. It is said that the intense, spicy fragrance of the sauce was like a siren's call to the men who visited "ladies of the night."

Cipolline are small onions, often called wild onions. For peak flavor, they should be braised or slowly simmered in olive oil.

Tagliatelle with Mushrooms, Cipollini Onions & Pancetta

Serves 6

Salt
Olive Oil
4 oz. pancetta, chopped
1 pint cipolline onions, peeled and halved
1 pound mushrooms, such as shiitakes or
creminis, sliced
2 garlic cloves, smashed with a knife
Needles from 1 small rosemary sprig
Cracked black pepper
1 pound tagliatelle or fettuccini
4 tablespoons cold unsalted butter,
cut into pieces
½ cup freshly grated Parmesan cheese,
plus extra for serving
Large handful of chopped, fresh, flat-leaf
parsley

1. Bring a large pot of salted water to a boil
   over high heat for pasta.

2. Heat 3 tablespoons olive oil in a large
   skillet over medium heat. Add pancetta
   and onions, cooking for 7 to 8 minutes
   to render fat and lightly brown onions.
   Add mushrooms, garlic and rosemary,
   and cook for about 12 minutes, until
   mushrooms are well caramelized. Season
   with salt and pepper; put the vegetables
   into a big serving bowl. Cover with a
   plate to keep warm.

3. Keep rendered fat in skillet for cooking the sauce.

4. Add the tagliatelle to boiling water. Stir
   to separate pasta strands. Cook until al
   dente, 8 to 9 minutes. When the pasta is
   about halfway cooked, scoop out about 1
   cup pasta water and add it to the skillet.

5. Put skillet over medium heat, add cold
   butter, and simmer for 8 to 10 minutes,
   until liquid is reduced and thickened to
   a smooth consistency.

6. Drain tagliatelle and add to the bowl with
   the mushrooms and onions. Pour in hot
   butter sauce. Add Parmesan, plenty of
   cracked black pepper and parsley. Toss
   and serve with more cheese.

Serves 8-10

2 tablespoons unsalted butter, plus more for buttering a baking dish

½ pound short, bite-size pasta such as penne, ziti, or shells

2 teaspoons sea salt

2 tablespoons olive oil

1 large yellow onion, diced

3 cloves garlic, minced

2 cups milk

2 cups heavy cream

3 ½ cups rotisserie roasted chicken, shredded

1 cup shredded sharp cheddar cheese

1 cup shredded sharp white cheddar cheese

½ cup grated Parmesan cheese

8 ounces fresh spinach, washed, stems removed and drained

2 tablespoons chopped fresh oregano

1 to 2 tablespoons hot sauce (Crystal brand is good)

2 teaspoons salt

1 teaspoon freshly ground black pepper

Maccheroni & Cheese
with Chicken & Spinach

1. Preheat oven to 350 degrees. Lightly butter a 9x13-inch baking dish.

2. Bring a large pot of lightly salted water to a boil. Add pasta, stir and cook until al dente. Drain in a colander and transfer pasta to a large bowl. Drizzle with 1 tablespoon of olive oil and toss to coat.

3. Melt butter with the remaining tablespoon of olive oil in a large skillet over medium heat. Add onion and cook, stirring occasionally for 3 to 4 minutes, until translucent. Add garlic and cook for 1 minute longer, stirring constantly so the garlic does not burn.

4. Stir in milk and cream, reduce heat to low, and simmer, stirring occasionally for about 20 minutes, until the sauce is reduced by half and is thick enough to coat the back of a spoon.

5. Remove the sauce from heat and add chicken, cheddars, Parmesan, spinach, oregano, hot sauce, salt and pepper. Stir

until cheeses have melted and spinach has wilted. Pour into the bowl with the pasta and toss to coat pasta with the sauce. Taste for salt and pepper; season with more to taste.

6. Transfer the pasta to the prepared baking dish, scraping the bowl with a spatula, and bake for about 45 minutes or until sauce is bubbling around the edges and the pasta is slightly brown on top. Remove from oven and let rest for about 10 minutes before serving. If using individual gratin dishes, reduce baking time to 30 minutes.

Mac & cheese is always a great opportunity to clean out your cheese drawer. Try a mixture of several cheeses.

Roasted Garlic & Wild Mushroom Risotto

Serves 6

2 large whole heads garlic
4 tablespoons olive oil
¾ ounce dried porcini mushrooms
¾ pound mixed fresh wild mushrooms
(shiitake, crimini) sliced
1 cup chopped shallots
2 tablespoons chopped fresh thyme
1 ½ cups Arborio rice
½ cup dry white wine
5 cups chicken broth
2 cups thinly sliced fresh spinach leaves
½ cup freshly grated Parmesan

1. Preheat the oven to 400 degrees.

2. Combine garlic and 2 tablespoons oil in a small baking dish. Cover with foil and bake about 45 minutes, until garlic is golden and tender when pierced with a small knife. Cool slightly; squeeze garlic out of bulb.

3. Place porcini mushrooms in a small bowl. Pour enough hot water over to cover. Let stand for about 30 minutes until soft.

Drain, saving porcini juice, squeeze dry and coarsely chop. Strain leftover porcini water to remove any remnants.

4. Heat 1 tablespoon oil in a large nonstick skillet over medium-high heat. Add fresh mushrooms and sauté until golden and juices evaporate, about 10 minutes. Add porcini and stir 1 minute. Season with salt and pepper; set aside.

5. Heat last tablespoon oil in a heavy sauce-pan over medium-high heat. Add shallots and thyme, and sauté until tender, for about 5 minutes. Add rice and stir to coat with shallot mixture. Add wine and cook until almost evaporated. Mix in garlic and 1 cup chicken broth. Bring to a boil. Reduce heat and continue to add broth, ½ cup at a time, stirring for about 20 minutes.

6. Add mushroom mixture and spinach. Stir until spinach wilts, then stir in Parmesan cheese. Season to taste with salt and pepper.

Gnocchi with Pesto

Serves 8

2 packages of vacuum packed gnocchi
2 tablespoons pine nuts
½ teaspoon salt
2 cloves garlic
1 teaspoon red pepper flakes
2 cups packed basil leaves
½ cup olive oil
2 tablespoons Parmesan
¼ cup heavy cream

1. Bring a large pot of water to boil; add salt, then gnocchi. The gnocchi will sink to the bottom of the pot. When they float to the top, cook for an additional 2 minutes.

2. Pulse pine nuts and ½ teaspoon salt together in a food processor until finely ground. Add garlic, red pepper flakes and basil and, with the motor running, drizzle in olive oil.

3. Warm the pesto over medium heat in a large skillet. Stir in cheese and cream. Add gnocchi, stir gently, and serve.

4. Shave additional Parmesan over the top.

Serves 6

1 ¼ cups canned pumpkin
2 tablespoons dry breadcrumbs
2 tablespoons fresh grated Parmesan cheese
½ teaspoon salt
½ teaspoon minced fresh sage
¼ teaspoon ground nutmeg
30 round wonton wrappers
1 tablespoon cornstarch
Cooking spray
1 cup milk
1 tablespoon all-purpose flour
1 ½ tablespoons butter
½ cup crumbled Gorgonzola cheese
3 tablespoons toasted walnuts

Make your own pasta, or take this short-cut using wonton wrappers.

Pumpkin Ravioli with
Gorgonzola Sauce & Toasted Walnuts

1. Spoon pumpkin onto several layers of heavy-duty paper towels, and spread to ½ inch thickness. Cover with additional paper towels; let stand 5 minutes. Scrape into a medium bowl using a rubber spatula. Stir in breadcrumbs, Parmesan, salt, minced sage, pepper and nutmeg.

2. Working with 1 wonton wrapper at a time (cover remaining wrappers with a damp towel to keep from drying out), spoon 2 teaspoons pumpkin mixture into center of wrapper. Brush edges of wrapper with water and fold in half, pressing edges firmly with fingers to form a half-moon.

3. Place on a large baking sheet sprinkled with cornstarch. Repeat procedure with remaining wonton wrappers and pumpkin mixture.

4. Fill a large pot with water and bring to a simmer. Add half of ravioli to pan (cover remaining ravioli with a damp towel). Cook 4 minutes or until done (do not boil), stirring gently. Remove ravioli with a slotted spoon; lightly coat with cooking spray, and keep warm. Repeat procedure with remaining ravioli.

5. Combine milk and flour in a saucepan, stirring with a whisk. Bring to a boil; cook for 1 minute or until thick, stirring constantly. Remove from heat. Add butter, stirring until butter melts. Gently stir in Gorgonzola.

6. Place 5 ravioli in each of 6 shallow bowls, and drizzle each serving with 3 tablespoons Gorgonzola sauce. Sprinkle each serving with 1 ½ teaspoons walnuts. Serve immediately.

Meatballs with Porcini Mushrooms & Pecorino

Serves 6

3 ounces dried porcini mushrooms, soaked in warm water for 30 minutes
1 ½ pounds ground beef
¼ cup freshly grated pecorino cheese
4 tablespoons chopped fresh parsley, plus extra to serve
2 garlic cloves, finely chopped
¾ cup fresh white breadcrumbs
3 tablespoons milk
1 egg, beaten
Salt and freshly ground black pepper
Olive oil for frying
Flour for coating

1. Drain mushrooms and chop finely. Put into a bowl with ground meat, pecorino, parsley and garlic. Mix together well. Soak the breadcrumbs in the milk. Squeeze until damp and add egg. Season with salt and pepper. Add to the meat-porcini mixture and combine until it comes together. Cover and chill in the refrigerator for 30 minutes.

2. Form the chilled meatball mixture into balls, roll in flour and fry in hot olive oil for about 3 minutes on each side until cooked through and golden brown. Add to basic marinara sauce and heat through.

3. Sprinkle with parsley, and then serve immediately.

Caramelized Squash-Filled Ravioli with Sage Butter

Serves 6

Sage Butter
1 stick of unsalted butter
1 bunch of fresh sage leaves, finely chopped
Additional leaves for garnish
Toasted pine nuts for garnish

1. Melt the butter in a small skillet. Add the sage and cook until slightly crisp and begins to sizzle.

1 recipe basic pasta dough
2 pounds butternut squash, skin and seeds removed
3 large eggs

Ravioli is a great first course. Make 3 large ones for each guest. For a nice finish, grate a little amaretti cookie on the top.

1. Cut squash into 2-inch chunks, toss lightly with olive oil, salt and pepper. Roast in a 450 degree oven for about 1 hour or until caramelized and tender. Stir squash occasionally during the roasting to prevent burning. Remove from the oven and cool.

2. Process in batches in the food processor until smooth. Add eggs one at a time to blend. Adjust seasoning to taste with additional salt and pepper. Refrigerate until ready to use.

3. Roll out the pasta dough. Place filling onto the dough and roll out a second piece of dough and cover, pressing down to secure and remove any air pockets. Using a ravioli wheel or pizza cutter, cut the ravioli into 3-inch squares.

4. In a large pot of boiling water, cook ravioli for 3 minutes, stirring gently to keep from sticking. Drain and arrange on a serving platter. Spoon with sage butter. Garnish with fresh sprigs of sage and toasted pine nuts.

Winter

Red Wine Spaghetti

Serves 8

1 pound spaghetti
1 bottle red wine (preferably Zinfandel)
1 teaspoon sugar
Salt
Freshly ground pepper
Olive oil for garnish

1. Bring a large pot of water to a boil and cook the spaghetti for 5 minutes (pasta will not be fully cooked.) Reserve 1 cup of pasta water and drain in colander; return empty pot to stovetop.

2. Add wine and sugar to pot and boil vigorously 2 minutes until liquid slightly reduces. Add spaghetti and shake pot to prevent pasta from sticking. Gently stir with tongs until coated; boil over high heat, stirring occasionally, until most of the wine is absorbed, about 6 minutes (pasta will become al dente.) If needed, add the reserved cup of pasta water.

3. Season with salt and pepper and drizzle with olive oil.

4. Serve immediately.

I've included a recipe for lamb to serve with the red-wine spaghetti. The dish will go well with any red meat, however.

Grilled Lamb Chops with Rosemary & Thyme

Serves 6

6 tablespoons olive oil
6 large garlic cloves
6 tablespoons fresh rosemary leaves, coarsely chopped
6 teaspoons fresh thyme leaves
2 teaspoons sea salt
Pinch of cayenne pepper
3 racks of lamb

1. Preheat the oven to 400 degrees.

2. In a food processor fitted with a metal blade, blend oil, garlic, rosemary, thyme, sea salt and cayenne pepper to form a paste. Rub paste over racks of lamb and marinate for at least 30 minutes, but up to 4 hours.

3. Heat a grill pan over a high flame. Add chops and sear for 2 minutes on each side. Transfer to the oven and roast for 20 minutes for medium rare. Transfer to plates.

4. Serve each person three chops.

Serve these lamb chops with the red-wine spaghetti; they taste great together.

Serves 8-10

⅓ cup plus ¼ cup olive oil
2 large zucchini, cut into planks and grilled with olive oil, cooled and cut into cubes
Salt and freshly ground black pepper
1 tablespoon minced garlic
1 pound spicy Italian sausage, casings removed or ground sausage
⅓ cup dry red wine

3 cups marinara sauce
1 teaspoon dried crushed red pepper flakes
8 ounces angel hair pasta
½ pound mozzarella, diced
1 cup freshly grated Parmesan cheese

Baked Angel Hair Pasta with
Grilled Zucchini & Spicy Italian Sausage in Puff Pastry

1. Heat $\frac{1}{3}$ cup olive oil, sauté garlic and add sausage and red wine. Cook over medium-high heat until wine has evaporated and the sausage is brown, breaking sausage into pieces with the back of a spoon, about 8 minutes. Add marinara sauce and crushed red pepper. Add the grilled zucchini to the pan.

2. Meanwhile, bring a large pot of salted water to a boil over high heat. Add angel hair and cook, stirring constantly, until pasta is still slightly crunchy and under-cooked, about 6 minutes. Drain. Toss angel hair with the zucchini mixture. Cool completely. Add mozzarella and Parmesan and toss to combine.

3. Preheat the oven to 375 degrees.

4. Roll out 1 pastry sheet on a floured surface to a 13 ½-inch square. Transfer to a 10-inch spring-form pan, letting excess pastry hang over the rim. Spoon pasta mixture into the pan. Place second pastry sheet on top of the pasta filling. Pinch edges of the pastry sheets together to seal.

5. Trim the overhanging pastry to 1-inch. Fold pastry edges to form a decorative border. Cut a slit in the center of the top pastry to allow steam to escape.

6. Bake pastry for 1 hour , or until pastry is brown and puffed on top. Let stand for 10 minutes, then remove the pan sides and serve. Brush top of the pastry with olive oil.

Invite people over and serve this pasta dish. It makes a great get-together dish.

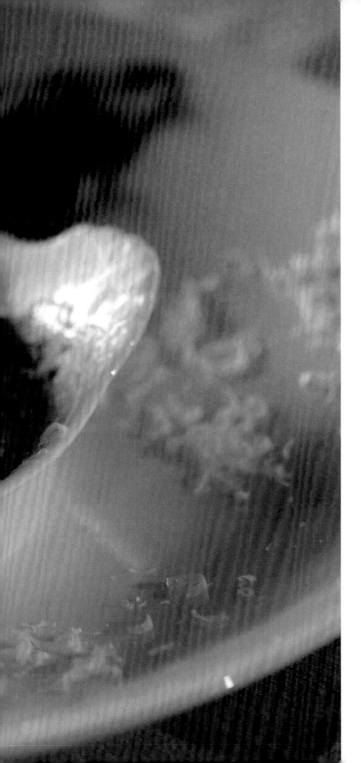

Florentine Cannelloni

Serves 8

Pasta
6 eggs, room temperature
1 ½ cups flour
1 ½ cups water

1. In a medium bowl, combine the eggs, flour and water using an electric mixer. Beat until just smooth; batter should not be frothy. Let stand 30 minutes or longer before using. Slowly heat an 8-inch skillet or crepe pan on low heat. Oil pan using a paper towel or brush. Pour in 3 tablespoons of batter, rotating skillet quickly to spread batter evenly over the bottom.

2. Cook pasta over low heat until the top is dry but the bottom is not brown. Turn out on a wire rack to cool. Continue cooking until all of batter is used. After the pasta has cooled, place each between sheets of waxed paper Pasta may be made a day in advance and refrigerated or frozen.

Filling

2 tablespoons olive oil
1 link hot Italian sausage
1 teaspoon finely chopped garlic
3 10-ounce packages frozen chopped spinach, defrosted and drained
5 tablespoons grated Parmesan cheese
2 tablespoons heavy cream
2 eggs lightly beaten
½ teaspoon dried oregano
Salt and freshly ground pepper

1. Heat olive oil in a 10-inch skillet. Add Italian sausage and cook thoroughly. Add onions and garlic, and cook over moderate heat, stirring frequently for about 8 minutes. Stir in spinach and cook for about 4 minutes more. When all of the moisture has boiled away and spinach sticks lightly to pan, transfer to a large bowl and let cool. Add cheese, cream, eggs and oregano. Season with salt and pepper.

Marinara Sauce

3 tablespoons olive oil
1 cup finely chopped onions
1 tablespoon finely chopped garlic
4 cups Italian plum tomatoes, coarsely chopped
1 six ounce can tomato paste
1 teaspoon red pepper flakes
1 tablespoon dried oregano
1 tablespoon fresh basil
1 bay leaf
2 teaspoons sugar
1 ½ teaspoons salt
Freshly ground black pepper

1. In a 4-quart saucepan, heat olive oil, add onions and cook over moderate heat for 10 minutes. When onions are soft and transparent, add garlic. Stir in tomatoes and their liquid, tomato paste, red pepper flakes, oregano, basil, bay leaf, sugar, salt and pepper. Bring the sauce to a boil, turn heat to very low and simmer uncovered for about 1 hour.

Besciamella Sauce

4 tablespoons butter
4 tablespoons flour
1 cup milk
1 cup heavy cream
1 teaspoon salt
⅛ teaspoon freshly ground black pepper

1. In a heavy 2-3 quart saucepan melt butter. Remove pan from the heat and stir in flour. Pour in milk and cream all at once, whisking constantly until the flour has dissolved.

2. Return the pan to high heat and cook, stirring constantly with a whisk. When the sauce comes to a boil and is smooth, reduce the heat. Sauce should be thick enough to coat the wires of whisk heavily. Remove from heat and season with salt and pepper.

Assembly

1. Preheat the oven to 350 degrees.

2. Fill each pasta with filling. Pour a thin film of tomato sauce on the bottom of the dish.

3. Lay cannelloni side by side in one layer on top of sauce. Pour besciamella over cannelloni and spoon remaining marinara sauce on the top.

4. Scatter 4 tablespoons grated Parmesan cheese over top of the dish and bake uncovered for 40 minutes until cheese is melted and sauce is bubbling. Serve from the baking dish.

5. Cannelloni may be made ahead of time and frozen.

Baked Penne with Four Cheeses

Serves 6

1 pound penne
¼ cup olive oil
2 cups heavy cream
1 ball fresh water-packed mozzarella cheese, sliced thin
2 ounces fontina cheese
2 counces Parmesan cheese
2 ounces gorgonzola cheese
1 cup chopped Roma tomatoes, seeds removed
5 leaves fresh basil, chiffonade
1 teaspoon salt
1 teaspoon black pepper

1. Bring four quarts of water to a rolling boil, add penne and cook until al dente about 10 minutes. Remove, drain and toss with olive oil.

2. Heat heavy cream on low heat. Shred or crumble cheeses and add to cream along with tomatoes, basil, salt and pepper.

3. Preheat oven to 450 degrees. Toss pasta with cheese mixture and spread evenly in a shallow casserole. Bake for 10 to 12 minutes until bubbly and the pasta is slightly charred on top. Serve immediately.

I like to serve this in individual gratin dishes as a side dish, or with a salad as an entree. Add some grilled ciabatta rubbed with a garlic clove for a complete meal.

Serves 8

1 pound eggplant (cubed)
1 ½ teaspoons salt, divided
1 ounce pancetta, chopped
2 cups thinly sliced onion
1 tablespoon olive oil
2 cloves garlic, thinly sliced
¼ cup dry white wine
1 tablespoon chopped fresh basil

1 teaspoon chopped fresh oregano
½ teaspoon crushed red pepper flakes
1 (28-ouce) can diced fire-roasted tomatoes, with juice
1 pound penne
1 cup shredded fontina cheese
1 (3-inch) piece French bread
½ cup grated fresh Parmesan cheese

Eggplant Marinara Pasta Gratin

1. Arrange the eggplant on several layers of paper towels. Sprinkle with 1 teaspoon salt; let stand 15 minutes. Pat dry.

2. Preheat oven to 450 degrees.

3. Arrange eggplant in a single layer on a baking sheet coated with cooking spray. Bake for 30 minutes or until lightly browned, stirring after 15 minutes. Remove from baking sheet; cool.

4. Cook pancetta over medium heat until crisp. Add onion, oil and garlic to pan; cook 5 minutes or until onion is lightly browned, stirring frequently. Add wine to pan; cook until liquid evaporates, scraping pan to loosen browned bits. Stir in basil, oregano, remaining ½ teaspoon salt, pepper, and diced tomatoes. Bring to a simmer over medium heat and cook for 20 minutes. Remove from the heat and stir in eggplant.

5. Cook pasta 10 minutes until al dente. Drain in a colander over a bowl, reserving ¼ cup cooking water. Add pasta and reserved water to tomato mixture; stir well. Spoon pasta mixture into a 9x13-inch baking dish coated with cooking spray. Sprinkle evenly with fontina.

6. Place French bread in a food processor; pulse until coarse crumbs measure 1 ½ cups. Add Parmesan to processor, and pulse a few times more. Sprinkle breadcrumb mixture evenly over fontina. Bake at 450 degrees for about 15 minutes or until cheese melts and begins to brown.

This make-ahead dish is great for the football season. Serve with caesar salad and crusty garlic bread, and you're ready for the game.

Take this basic mac & cheese recipe and add other ingredients.
Make it with four cheeses, add cooked pancetta or top with sliced
tomatoes. This one is always great and the possibilities are endless!

James Beard's Macaroni & Cheese

Serves 6

4 tablespoons butter
4 tablespoons flour
2 cups milk
Freshly ground black pepper
½ teaspoon hot sauce (Crystal)
½ cup heavy cream or creme fraiche
½ pound macaroni or elbows
¾ pound grated Cheddar cheese

1. Melt butter in a saucepan. Add flour, and stir until the roux is frothy and the taste of raw flour is gone. Meanwhile, heat milk in another pan. Add warmed milk gradually to the roux, stirring continuously. Turn up heat and cook, stirring, until the sauce is just at the boiling point.

2. Turn down the heat and let it simmer for a few minutes. Add the pepper and hot sauce. Stir in cream and simmer a little longer, until all flavors are blended.

3. Cook the pasta just until al dente. Drain.

4. Preheat oven to 350 degrees.

5. Mix three-quarters of the grated cheese into the simmering sauce. As soon as it melts, combine with drained macaroni and pour into a baking pan. Sprinkle the top with remaining cheese, and bake for 30 minutes.

Serves 6

3 tablespoons olive oil
2 ounces pancetta, chopped (about ½ cup)
2 ½ pounds of short ribs
Salt and freshly ground black pepper
¼ cup all-purpose flour
1 medium onion, chopped
1 carrot, peeled and chopped
½ cup fresh flat-leaf parsley leaves
2 cloves garlic
1 14-ounce can tomatoes, whole or diced
1 tablespoon tomato paste
1 teaspoon chopped fresh rosemary
½ teaspoon red pepper flakes
1 teaspoon dried thyme
½ teaspoon dried oregano
1 bay leaf
2 ½ cups beef broth
¾ cup red wine
Salt and pepper to taste
1 pound fresh or dried tagliatelle
Parmesan cheese for grating

Tagliatelle with Short Rib Ragu

1. Heat olive oil in a large, heavy soup pot over medium heat. Cook pancetta until golden and crisp, about 4 minutes.

2. Meanwhile, season short ribs with salt and pepper, and lightly coat with flour. Using a slotted spoon, remove pancetta from the pan and set it aside. Add short ribs to the pan and cook until browned on all sides, about 7 minutes total. Meanwhile, combine the onion, carrot, parsley, garlic, tomatoes and tomato paste in a food processor and pulse until finely minced.

3. Once the short ribs are browned, add the minced vegetables to the pot along with the pancetta and stir. Add rosemary, red pepper flakes, thyme, oregano, bay leaf, beef broth and wine. Bring mixture to a boil, then reduce heat, cover and simmer for 1 hour and 15 minutes. Remove the lid and simmer for another hour and 30 minutes, stirring occasionally.

4. Using a slotted spoon lift out the short ribs and let cool briefly on a plate. Shred the meat and return it to the pot, discarding bones and bay leaf. Add ½ teaspoon salt and ¾ teaspoon pepper. If necessary, reduce the sauce before adding meat and skim off fat.

5. Bring a large pot of salted water to a boil over high heat. Add pasta and cook until tender but still firm to the bite, stirring occasionally for 8 to 10 minutes. Drain, reserving 1 cup of cooking liquid.

6. Add pasta to the pot with short rib ragu and stir to combine. If needed, add reserved pasta liquid ¼ cup at a time to moisten the pasta. Transfer to serving bowl and top each with freshly grated Parmesan cheese.

Gemelli with Spicy Winter Squash, Applewood-Smoked Bacon & Spinach

Serves 8

¼ cup plus 2 tablespoons olive oil
6 large cloves garlic, thinly sliced
1 large red onion, thinly sliced
2 teaspoons crushed red pepper
8 ounces applewood-smoked bacon, cut into 1-inch pieces
2 pounds roasted butternut squash
6 ounces baby spinach
1 tablespoon finely chopped thyme
Salt and freshly ground pepper
1 ½ pounds gemelli or small pasta shells
¾ cup freshly grated pecorino or Parmesan cheese, plus more for serving

This is a great winter side dish with grilled pork tenderloin.

1. Bring a large pot of salted water to a boil.

2. In a large, deep skillet, heat olive oil. Add garlic, onion and crushed red pepper and cook over moderately high heat, stirring occasionally, until softened, about 5 minutes. Cook bacon until the fat is rendered and just turning crisp. Add squash, spinach, thyme, and season with salt and pepper; cook for 5 minutes, stirring occasionally. Continue cooking over moderately low heat, stirring occasionally until hot. Drain.

3. Meanwhile, add gemelli to boiling water and cook until al dente. Drain pasta, reserving 1 cup of pasta water. Add gemelli to squash mixture in the skillet, then stir in ½ cup pasta cooking water and toss gently to combine. Add cheese, season with salt and pepper and stir gently; add more pasta water if necessary. Serve pasta right away, passing more cheese at the table.

Serves 8-10

Meat Ragu

1-2 ounces dried porcini mushrooms
2 tablespoons olive oil
3 tablespoons butter
1 small red onion
3 carrots
2 celery ribs
2 cloves garlic
1 ½ pounds ground beef
⅓ pound ground pork
2 ounces pancetta
1 cup dry red wine
2 28-ounce cans Italian pureed tomatoes
1 tablespoon tomato paste
2 cups meat stock
Bouquet garni (sage, rosemary, thyme, bay leaves, wrapped with string)
Salt and freshly ground black pepper

This lasagne recipe is from the grand-mother of Fabio, our chef in Lucca. He really didn't have a recipe, so he asked me to watch him and write it out. It really is delicious. Usually we think of lasagne as a heavy dish. This is light.

Besciamella Sauce

4 tablespoons butter
4 tablespoons flour
2 cups milk
½ cup heavy cream
½ cup Parmesan cheese

Fresh or packaged lasagna noodles
Fresh mozzarella

1. Place mushrooms in warm water to soak, covered.

2. Using a grinder attachment for a stand mixer, grind onion, carrots, celery, ground beef and pork together. If not, finely chop all vegetables by hand or in a food processor.

3. Meanwhile, melt butter in olive oil over medium heat in a heavy casserole and add onion, carrots and celery. Cook for 5 to 10 minutes until golden, but not brown. Add meat and pancetta, and continue to brown lightly. Add wine, turn up

heat and boil until evaporated. Reduce heat, and then add pureed tomatoes and tomato paste. Mix well, then add stock and bouquet garni.

4. Bring to a boil, stir well, then half cover and simmer for about 3 hours, topping with a little water to prevent drying out. Skim any fat off the top if desired.

5. After 1 ½ hours, drain mushrooms, reserving liquid, chop finely and add to sauce. Stir well, add some of the mushroom water and continue to simmer. The sauce should be very thick and rich. Season well.

6. To make the béchamel sauce, melt butter in a saucepan. Add flour and stir until smooth and the taste of raw flour is gone. Meanwhile, heat milk in another pan. Add warm milk gradually to the roux, stirring all the while. Turn up heat and cook, stirring, until the sauce is just at the boiling point. Reduce heat and let simmer for a few minutes. Stir in heavy cream, Parmesan cheese and simmer a little longer, until the flavors are blended.

Assembly

1. Preheat the oven to 375 degrees.

2. Spray or butter a large casserole dish. Put down a thin layer of meat sauce. Put a layer of lasagna and top with béchamel. Repeat ending with béchamel and then sauce on top. Slice mozzarella and place on top of the sauce. Bake 30 minutes or until heated through and bubbling.

3. Serve grated Parmesan on the side.

Fettuccine with Gorgonzola & Walnut Sauce

Serves 6

2 tablespoons butter
5 shallots, finely chopped
1 tablespoon plus 2 teaspoons chopped
fresh thyme
2 cups heavy cream
½ pound Gorgonzola cheese, crumbled
Freshly ground pepper
1 pound freshly made fettuccine
1 cup walnuts, coarsely
chopped and toasted
½ cup freshly grated Parmesan cheese

1. Melt butter in a heavy skillet over medium heat. Add shallots and sauté until translucent, about 5 minutes.

2. Stir in thyme. Add cream and Gorgonzola; stir until cheese melts and the sauce thickens slightly.

3. Cook pasta in a large pot of rapidly boiling water until al dente. Drain well.

4. Return pasta to the pot, add sauce and stir over low heat until pasta is coated. Mix in the walnuts.

5. Transfer to a serving dish and sprinkle with cheese.

Homemade fettuccine turns this recipe into a light, delicious, creamy extravaganza. Look for Gorgonzola dolce. It's creamier, has more flavor, and melts well.

Pasta with Vodka Sauce

Serves 6

1 pound penne or other tubular pasta
5 tablespoons unsalted butter
⅔ cup vodka
¼ teaspoon hot red pepper flakes
1 can imported Italian plum tomatoes, drained and pureed
¾ cup heavy cream
½ teaspoon salt
¾ cup freshly grated Parmesan cheese
¼ cup Italian parsley, finely chopped for garnish

1. In a large pot of boiling water, cook penne until al dente, 8 to 10 minutes.

2. Meanwhile, melt butter in a large skillet over moderate heat. Add vodka and hot pepper flakes, simmering for 2 minutes. Add pureed tomatoes and cream, and then simmer for 5 minutes longer. Season with salt.

3. When pasta is al dente, drain well and pour into the skillet with the heated sauce. Reduce heat to low, add cheese and mix thoroughly. Pour into a heated bowl and serve at once with chopped parsley on top.

This classic pasta is served in Roman kitchens regularly. It is always a first course.

Spaghettini with Sun-Dried Tomato Pesto & Arugula

Serves 6

¾ cup plump, moist sun-dried tomatoes
1 - 2 cloves garlic
½ teaspoon red chili pepper flakes
¼ cup olive oil
Salt
1-pound box imported spaghettini
2 bunches arugula, trimmed and
coarsely chopped
Freshly grated Parmesan cheese

1. In a food processor with a steel blade, process sun-dried tomatoes with garlic, red chili pepper flakes and olive oil until mixture has a rough pesto texture. Scrape out mixture and transfer to a small bowl; add salt to taste.

2. Cook the spaghettini in boiling water until al dente. Drain.

3. Place pasta in a warmed serving bowl and toss with pesto until lightly coated.

4. Sprinkle with chopped arugula, toss again, and serve with Parmesan cheese.

If you buy sun-dried tomatoes in oil, drain and rinse well before putting in the food processor. The pesto's consistency will be better.

Spring

Spaghettini Primavera with Grilled Sea Scallops

Serves 6

1 pound sea scallops (Use paper towels to press out excess moisture)
¼ cup olive oil
1 tablespoon minced garlic
1 ½ cups diced onions
1 ½ cups diced tomatoes
1 ¼ teaspoon fresh oregano
2 teaspoons fresh basil
1 ½ teaspoons salt
½ teaspoons pepper
½ cup white wine
¼ cup drained capers
2 cups zucchini, cut into half moons
2 cups sliced shiitake mushrooms
⅓ cup chopped flat-leaf parsley
1 pound spaghettini, cooked al dente
4 Roma tomatoes, seeded and chopped for garnish
Parmesan cheese

1. Preheat a barbecue or stove top grill. Toss sea scallops with olive oil and grill until just cooked through.

2. Sauté garlic, onions and tomatoes in ¼ cup olive oil. Simmer until just soft.

3. Add all herbs, spices, white wine, capers, zucchini and mushrooms. Cook just until tender. Add parsley and toss with spaghettini.

4. Place pasta on a large platter and arrange grilled scallops on top. Garnish with chopped tomatoes and freshly grated Parmesan cheese.

Primavera means "spring style" and refers to the use of fresh vegetables. Feel free to substitute any vegetables in season and shrimp or halibut in place of the scallops.

Spaghettini with Asparagus, Shiitake Mushrooms, Lemon & Chives

Serves 6

1 pound spaghettini
4 tablespoons butter, divided
2 tablespoons olive oil
½ cup thinly sliced shallots
1 pound fresh shiitake mushrooms, stemmed, sliced
6 tablespoons fresh lemon juice
1 ¾ cups chicken broth
1 tablespoon grated lemon zest
1 pound asparagus, tough ends trimmed, cut crossswise into thirds
¼ cup chopped fresh chives
4 ounces shaved Asiago cheese

Asiago is a semi-firm Italian cheese with a rich, nutty flavor. It adds a lot of taste to this dish.

1. Cook spaghettini in a large pot of boiling salted water until tender but still firm to bite, stirring occasionally. Drain. Transfer pasta to large wide bowl.

2. Meanwhile, melt 2 tablespoons butter with oil in heavy large skillet over medium heat. Add shallots; sauté for 1 minute. Add shiitake mushrooms; sprinkle with salt and pepper. Sauté shiitake mixture until soft, about 6 minutes. Add lemon juice; cook 1 minute.

3. Add broth and lemon zest and bring to a boil. Reduce heat to medium and simmer until liquid is reduced by half, about 6 minutes. Add asparagus to shiitake mixture; simmer until asparagus turns bright green, about 2 minutes. Add chives and remaining 2 tablespoons butter and stir until butter melts. Season sauce to taste with salt and pepper.

4. Pour sauce over pasta; toss to coat. Top with shaved Asiago and serve.

Pearl Couscous with Grilled Zucchini

Serves 6

3 cups chicken stock
1 teaspoon salt
1 teaspoon freshly ground black pepper
1 ½ cups pearl couscous
1 teaspoon garlic, minced
1 tablespoon fresh chives, chopped
1 tablespoon fresh rosemary, chopped
1 tablespoon fresh basil, chopped
1 tablespoon fresh mint, chopped
2 medium zucchini, sliced on the diagonal
1 bunch scallions
1 tablespoon olive oil
½ cup Pecorino Romano, grated

1. Bring chicken stock to a boil and mix in the salt and pepper. Add couscous and cook until chicken stock is absorbed, about 10 minutes.

2. Mix herbs and garlic together and allow to sit until ready to serve the couscous.

3. Grill the zucchini and scallions on a grill or in a non-stick grill pan. Chop into bite size pieces.

4. Stir the couscous, add the herbs, garlic, zucchini and scallions and serve immediately. Grate cheese over the top.

Great side dish for grilled halibut or chicken!

Lemon & Black Pepper Fettuccine with Scallions

Serves 6

1 8-ounce package fresh fettucine
¼ minced shallot
3 cloves garlic, thinly sliced
1 tablespoon butter
1 8-ounce container of mascarpone
4 tablespoons freshly grated Parmesan, divided
1 tablespoon cream
Juice and zest of one lemon
1 teaspoon freshly ground black pepper
2 tablespoons freshly chopped chives

1. Cook fettucine in boiling salted water until al dente. Keep warm while preparing sauce.

2. In a large skillet, sauté shallots and garlic in butter, stirring until tender, but not brown. Add mascarpone, 2 tablespoons Parmesan cheese, cream, lemon zest and juice, 1 teaspoon freshly ground black pepper and salt. Cook until heated through for about 4 minutes.

3. Add cooked fettucine to pan with chopped chives and remaining Parmesan. Add more pepper to taste if necessary and toss well. Serve with crusty bread.

If available, Meyer lemons are great in this pasta. They are a little sweet, so really great with lots of black pepper.

Serves 4-6

¾ pound dried spaghettini
¾ pound zucchini (slice using a vegetable peeler or a V-Slicer, the fatter the zucchini the better)
Salt and freshly ground pepper
½ cup olive oil
2 tablespoons minced garlic
½ teaspoon red pepper flakes
3 tablespoons coarsely chopped fresh basil
2 tablespoons finely chopped fresh flat-leaf parsley
½ cup plus 2 tablespoons freshly grated Parmesan cheese

1. Bring a large pot of water to a boil and add salt. Add pasta and cook until al dente, about 10 minutes.

2. While water comes to a boil and pasta cooks, cut zucchini on a mandoline or V-Slicer (otherwise slice to a fine julienne.) Season with salt and pepper. Very fine zucchini will not need additional cooking, but if slightly thick, place in a colander, suspend over pasta pot, cover and steam zucchini until still slightly crunchy, about 2 minutes.

3. Heat ¼ cup olive oil in a small skillet over medium-high heat until hot. Add garlic and sauté briefly until light brown. Add red pepper flakes. Quickly add basil and parsley, mix well, and remove from heat.

4. When pasta is al dente, drain, reserving about ½ cup of the pasta cooking water. Pour pasta in a warm serving bowl, add zucchini, the remaining ¼ cup oil, garlic mixture, and ½ cup of the cheese. Toss well, adding cooking water as needed to make a smooth sauce.

5. Taste for seasoning and add salt and pepper as needed. Sprinkle with the remaining 2 tablespoons Parmesan and serve at once.

Spaghettini with Olive Oil, Garlic & Julienne of Zucchini

Risotto Primavera Mold

Serves 6

6 cups chicken or vegetable stock
½ cup butter
3 green onions, chopped
2 ¼ cups Arborio rice
1 cup shelled green peas
½ cup asparagus tips, diced
½ cup string beans, diced
1 ½ cups carrots, diced
1 tablespoon minced fresh chives
1 tablespoon minced fresh flat-leaf
(Italian) parsley
Salt
2 tablespoons olive oil
6 tomatoes, peeled, seeded and diced

1. Preheat an oven to 400 degrees.

2. Pour stock into a saucepan and bring to a simmer over very low heat. Coat a 9-inch ring mold with 1 tablespoon butter and set aside.

3. Melt half of the remaining butter in a heavy saucepan over medium heat. Add onions and cook, stirring, until translucent, about 3 minutes. Add rice and cook, stirring, for about 2 minutes.

4. Add about 2 cups of simmering stock and continue to stir. Continue adding stock, a ladleful at a time, allowing most of the liquid to be absorbed before adding the next. Make sure that the rice is always covered with a thin layer of stock. After 9 minutes, add peas, asparagus, beans and carrots and cook for 3 minutes, allowing the mixture to become dry slightly.

5. Remove rice from the heat and add remaining butter, chives, parsley and salt. Stir well and pour mixture into the prepared mold. Transfer mold to preheated oven and bake for 5 minutes.

6. While the mold is in the oven, heat oil in a frying pan over medium-high heat and add tomatoes. Sauté until heated through, only a few minutes. When the mold is ready, run a knife blade around the edges to loosen, then invert onto a platter. Fill the hollow center with the tomatoes and serve immediately.

Spaghettini All'Amatriciana with Bruschetta

Serves 6

3 tablespoons olive oil
6 ounces pancetta, finely diced
½ - ¾ teaspoon dried red pepper flakes
2 cups finely chopped tomatoes
2 tablespoons freshly grated Parmigiano-Reggiano
1 cup freshly grated Pecorino-Romano
Salt
1 pound spaghettini

1. Bring a large pot of water to a boil over high heat. Meanwhile, heat oil in a large skillet over medium heat. Add pancetta and cook until browned and crisp, about 10 minutes. Then transfer with a slotted spoon to paper towels to drain, and set aside.

2. Increase heat to medium-high, carefully add red pepper flakes and tomatoes to hot oil in same pan and cook, stirring often, until sauce thickens slightly, about 10 minutes. Reduce heat to medium, add Parmigiano-Reggiano and 2 tablespoons of Pecorino-Romano. Cook for a few minutes longer.

3. Season the boiling water generously with salt, add spaghettini and cook, stirring often until just tender, about 8 minutes. Drain.

4. Transfer pasta to skillet with sauce, add 2-3 tablespoons Pecorino and stir until well coated. Divide spaghettini between bowls and sprinkle each with some reserved pancetta and a bit more Pecorino.

Bruschetta

To make classic bruschetta as it's done in Rome, grill thick slices of country-style Italian bread over medium-hot coals (or under a broiler) until browned and slightly charred in places. Remove bread slices from grill, lightly rub each side with just enough of 1 peeled garlic clove to perfume the bread, then brush each side with some olive oil. Sprinkle with a little salt and freshly ground black pepper, if desired.

Lemon Pepper Orzo with Mascarpone & Grilled Asparagus

Serves 6

2 ½ cups chicken stock
1 cup orzo
2 lemons, juice and zest
¼ cup cream
¼ cup grated Parmesan
2 tablespoons mascarpone cheese
2 tablespoons butter
1 pound asparagus, grilled and cut into
1-inch pieces
2 tablespoons fresh chives
1 tablespoon freshly ground black pepper

1. In a medium saute pan, bring the chicken stock to a boil. Add the orzo and cook for about 8 minutes, until liquid is almost absorbed and orzo is tender. Turn the heat off.

2. Stir in the asparagus and all of the remaining ingredients. Season with salt and pepper.

3. Serve as a side dish or on its own with a salad.

Mac & Cheese Carbonara

Serves 6

1 tablespoon olive oil
1-inch thick piece pancetta, cut to small dice
3 cloves garlic, finely chopped
3 tablespoons all-purpose flour
6 to 7 cups whole milk, heated
4 large egg yolks, lightly whisked
2 teaspoons finely chopped
fresh thyme leaves
1 teaspoon cayenne pepper
2 cups freshly grated Asiago cheese,
plus more for the top

1 ½ cups Irish white Cheddar,
plus more for the top
1 ½ cups grated Fontina cheese,
plus more for the top
½ cup freshly grated Parmesan,
plus more for the top
Salt and freshly ground black pepper
1 pound elbow macaroni, cooked just
under al dente
½ cup coarsely chopped flat-leaf parsley

1. Pre-heat oven to 350 degrees. Butter bottom and sides of a 3-quart baking dish and set aside.

2. Heat the oil in a large sauté pan over medium heat. Add pancetta and cook until golden brown on all sides. Remove with a slotted spoon to a plate lined with paper towels.

3. Add garlic to the pan and cook until lightly golden brown. Whisk in flour and cook for 1 to 2 minutes. Whisk in 6 cups hot milk, increase heat to high and cook, whisking constantly until thickened for 3 to 5 minutes. Whisk in eggs until incorporated and let cook for 1 to 2 minutes.

4. Remove from heat and whisk in thyme, cayenne, and all cheeses until completely melted; season with salt and pepper. If mixture is too thick, add some of the remaining milk ¼ cup at a time.

5. Place cooked macaroni in a large bowl, add cheese sauce, reserved pancetta and parsley and stir until combined. Transfer the mixture to the prepared pan. Combine together additional Asiago, Cheddar, Fontina and Parmesan in a bowl and sprinkle evenly over the top of the macaroni. Bake until heated through and the top is lightly golden brown, about 15 minutes. Remove from the oven and let rest 10 minutes before serving.

Poblano Chile Macaroni with Corn

Serves 4

1 tablespoon corn oil
¼ cup diced poblano chile
¼ cup diced red bell pepper
¼ cup diced red onion
1 tablespoon minced garlic
½ cup sweet white corn kernels
2 cups cooked elbow macaroni
½ cup roasted, peeled and pureed poblano chile
¾ cup heavy cream
½ cup grated hot pepper Jack cheese
Salt and cracked black pepper to taste

1. Heat corn oil in a heavy pan over high heat and sauté diced poblano chile, red bell pepper, red onion and garlic until just tender.

2. Add the corn kernels and sauté quickly.

3. Add the macaroni, poblano mixture, cream and pepper Jack cheese. Stir until all the ingredients are thoroughly mixed. Season to taste and serve.

This is a great side dish to serve with grilled pork tenderloin or chicken. So good . . .

Spaghetti Primavera

Serves 6

1 pound spaghetti
3 tablespoons olive oil
1 shallot, thinly sliced
2 cloves garlic, thinly sliced
½ teaspoon red pepper flakes
1 carrot, julienned into long strips
1 zucchini, julienned into long strips
1 yellow squash, julienned into long strips
1 Japanese eggplant, julienned into long strips
3 tablespoons butter
¼ cup chopped parsley
2 tablespoons chopped mint

1. Bring a large pot of water to a boil. Add salt and cook pasta until al dente, about 10 minutes.

2. In a large sauté pan, heat olive oil. Sauté shallot, garlic and red pepper flakes until soft, about 3 minutes.

3. Add the vegetables and continue sautéing for about 5 more minutes.

4. Lift spaghetti out of the boiling water and add to the skillet with the vegetables. Gently toss together.

5. Add butter, parsley and mint. Toss again and serve immediately.

A vegetable peeler works really well for cutting the vegetables into thin strips.

Orecchiette with Broccoli & Lemon-Parmesan Cream

Serves 6

1 pound orecchiette
½ pound broccoli florets
4 tablespoons butter
4 tablespoons fresh lemon juice
1 ⅓ cups heavy cream
Freshly ground pepper
1 cup freshly grated Parmesan cheese
½ cup minced fresh chives
4 teaspoons finely grated lemon zest

1. Bring a large pot of water to a boil. Add orecchiette and cook for about 10 minutes, stirring often, until al dente. Remove and add broccoli florets for 4-5 minutes. Drain. Return pasta and broccoli to the pot.

2. Meanwhile, in a small saucepan, melt butter, lemon juice and cream over moderately low heat. Reduce heat to very low, and cook until the cream is barely simmering for about 10 minutes.

3. Just before serving, stir the sauce into the pasta.

4. Add Parmesan, chives and lemon zest; season with salt and pepper and toss.

Orecchiette means "little ears" in Italian. Holds the sauce for every bite.

Pairings

The "For Every Season" series will include the recipes from my collection that can be matched up for infinite meal possibilities. Here are my favorites from the first book, *For Every Season, There is a Salad*, paired with a few recipes from this volume.

Crusty Pizza Bread with Gorgonzola Caesar Salad and Nonna's Lasagna

Caprese Salad Napoleons and
Fettuccine with Grilled Lobster Tails

Zucchini Carpaccio
and Tagliatelle with Short Rib Ragu

Glossary

Al dente - An Italian phrase meaning "to the tooth;" used to describe pasta that is cooked only until it offers a slight resistance when bitten into, but is not soft or overdone.

Asiago - A semi-firm Italian cheese with a rich, nutty flavor. It's made from whole or part skim cow's milk.

Anchovy - These tiny fish are generally filleted, salt-cured, and canned in oil.

Balsamic - This exquisite vinegar is made from white Trebbiano grape juice. It acquires its dark color and pungent sweetness from the process of aging in barrels of various woods, and graduating sizes, over a period of years.

Bechamel - This white sauce is made by stirring milk into a butter-flour roux.

Capers - The flower bud of a bush native to the Mediterranean. The small buds are picked, sun-dried and then pickled in vinegar brine.

Caramelize - To heat sugar until it liquefies and becomes a clear syrup; ranges in color from golden to dark brown.

Chiffonade - Refers to strips or shreds of vegetables lightly sautéed or used raw as a garnish.

Colby - A mild, whole milk cheese that has a softer texture and milder flavor than cheddar.

Feta - A classic Greek cheese traditionally made of sheep's or goat's milk. It is cured and stored in its own salty whey brine. Feta has a rich, tangy flavor.

Fontina - One of Italy's great cheeses. Semi-firm, yet creamy, it is a cow's milk cheese. The mild, nutty flavor, and the fact that it melts easily and smoothly, makes fontina perfect for any use.

Goat cheese - Pure white goat's milk cheese with a tart flavor. The texture ranges from moist and creamy to dry and semi-firm.

Gorgonzola - An ivory-colored interior, that can be lightly or thickly streaked with bluish-green veins, tells you it's Gorgonzola. This cow's milk cheese is rich and creamy with savory, slightly pungent flavor.

Kalamata olives - An almond-shaped Greek olive with a flavor that can be rich and fruity. They are packed in either olive oil or vinegar.

Mascarpone - A buttery-rich double cream to triple-cream cheese made from cow's milk. Ivory colored, soft and delicate.

Meyer lemons - A cross between a lemon and an orange. The aromatic juice is sweeter and less acidic than that of regular lemons. Meyer lemons are available in most areas from November through April.

Pancetta - An Italian bacon that is cured with salt and spices, but is not smoked. Flavorful and slightly salty, pancetta comes in a sausage-like roll. It is used to flavor sauces and pasta dishes.

Parmesan - This hard, dry cheese is made from skimmed or partially skimmed cow's milk. The complex flavor and granular texture are the results of a long aging process.

Pearl couscous - Couscous is a granular semolina, and pearl couscous is fatter than the original.

Pecorino romano - This cheese comes in large cylinders with a hard yellow rind and yellowish-white interior. It's good for grating.

Pesto - An uncooked sauce made with fresh basil, garlic, pine nuts, Parmesan cheese and olive oil. The ingredients are crushed with a mortar and pestle or finely chopped in a food processor.

Pine nuts - Also called pignoli this high-fat nut comes from several varieties of pine trees. The nuts are actually inside the pine cone, which generally must be heated to facilitate removal. The nutmeat is ivory colored.

Piquillo peppers - Piquant fired roasted peppers that are not spicy but have a touch of sweetness and a rich, roasted taste.

Polenta - A staple of northern Italy, polenta is a mush made from cornmeal. It can be eaten hot or cooled until firm, cut into squares and fried.

Puttanesca - A spicy mélange of tomatoes, onions, capers, black olives, anchovies, oregano and garlic, all cooked together in olive oil.

Red pepper flakes - A generic term applied to any of several varieties of hot, red chiles.

Risotto - An Italian rice dish specially made by stirring hot stock into a mixture of rice that has been sautéed. The stock is added a cup at a time and stirred continually while it cooks until all of the liquid is absorbed.

White cheddar - A firm cow's milk cheese that ranges in flavor from milky to sharp.

Index

Lemon Pepper Orzo with Mascarpone & Grilled Asparagus 151
Tiger Prawns & Spicy Roasted Red Pepper Pasta 82

P

Pancetta
  Gnocchi with Asparagus & Pancetta 87
  Tagliatelle with Mushrooms, Cipollini Onions & Pancetta 93
Pappardelle
  Pappardelle with Zucchini, Anchovies and Mint 51
Pearl Couscous
  Pearl Couscous with Grilled Zucchini 142
Penne
  Baked Penne with Four Cheeses 118
  Eggplant Marinara Pasta Gratin 121
  Pasta with Vodka Sauce 132
  Penne Zucchini Carbonara
Pesto
  Arugula Pesto 38
  Baked Lasagne with Asparagus & Pesto 84
  Basil Pesto 39
  Gnocchi with Pesto 99
  Grilled Vegetable Lasagne with Spicy Tomato-Olive Sauce & Pesto Oil 59
  Pesto Pizza 61
  Spaghettini with Sun-Dried Tomato Pesto & Arugula 135
  Sun-Dried Tomato Pesto 40
Piquillo Peppers
  Fettuccine with Creamy Piquillo Pepper-Feta Sauce 81
Pizza
  Pesto Pizza 61
Porcini
  Meatballs with Porcini Mushrooms & Pecorino 103

Buona
Fortuna